THE Pupil OF THE Eye

African Americans in the World Order of Bahá'u'lláh

Selections from the Writings of
Bahá'u'lláh, the Báb
'Abdu'l-Bahá, Shoghi Effendi,
and the Universal House of Justice

Compiled by Bonnie J. Taylor

Palabra Publications

Copyright © by Bonnie Taylor
ISBN 1-890101-00-1
First published September 1995
Second edition published 1998
Compiled by Bonnie J. Taylor

Palabra Publications
3735 B Shares Place
Rivera Beach, Florida 33404
USA
561-845-1919
561-845-0126 (fax)
palabrapub@aol.com

Contents

Notes and Acknowledgments v

The Pupil vii

One: People of African Descent 3
    I. Qualities and Characteristics 3
    II. Individual Bahá'ís of African Descent 9

Two: Race 21
    I. Origins of Racial Characteristics 21
    II. Measurement of Human Intelligence, Capacity and Worth 24
    III. The Intellect and Race 28

Three: Bahá'u'lláh's Principle of the Oneness of Mankind 33
    I. The Fundamental Principle of the Bahá'í Faith 33
    II. Eliminating Prejudices: Prerequisite to Unity and Peace 43
    III. The Danger of Prejudice and Disunity 50

Four: Unity in Diversity 61
    I. The Purpose and Value of Diversity 61
    II. The Principle of Unity in Diversity 67
    III. Maintaining Diversity 71

Five: Applying Solutions to Racism 75

    I. The Most Vital and Challenging Issue: Goal and Responsibilities 75

    II. Responsibilities of the Bahá'ís of European Descent 97

    III. Responsibilities of the Bahá'ís of African Descent 103

    IV. Reliance Upon Divine Power and the Love of God 110

    V. The Standard of Faith During Tests and Adversities 121

    VI. Justice—in Principle and Application 134

Six: African Americans and Teaching the Faith of Bahá'u'lláh 147

    I. Offering the Message of Bahá'u'lláh to People of African Ancestry 147

    II. The Need for Perseverance, Courage and Wisdom 153

    III. African Americans as Teachers of the Faith in America 159

    IV. Teaching and Serving in the African American Community 162

    V. Conferences and Committees 172

    VI. African Americans as Pioneers 179

Seven: Destiny 189

Bibliography 199

Notes and Acknowledgments

The Revelation proclaimed by Bahá'u'lláh was directed to the whole of mankind, and is universal in its scope. "The Ancient Beauty hath consented to be bound with chains," Bahá'u'lláh declared, "that mankind may be released from its bondage, and hath consented to be made a prisoner within this most mighty Stronghold that the whole world may attain unto true liberty."

While the Revelation of Bahá'u'lláh is universal, however, there are references to specific groups of people, including people of African descent. The writings of 'Abdu'l-Bahá, Shoghi Effendi and The Universal House of Justice also contain numerous such references, as well as a great deal of material written to and about African Americans in particular. This compilation endeavors to collect and organize as much of that material as possible.

Additional support material has also been included which, although it may not specifically refer to people of African ancestry, nevertheless elaborates upon many of the issues discussed in the quotations written about them. These support materials address experiences common to all human groups.

The writings specifically about African Americans that are contained herein describe their crucial and indispensable role in the Cause of God. It is hoped that this compilation will serve as an assistance to them as they struggle to overcome the difficulties in their path, and attain their goal and destiny in the new World Order.

I am deeply grateful to my husband, Clayton E. Taylor, Jr., and all the other African Americans who lovingly welcomed me into their homes and hearts. Their patient education, insight and wisdom in issues of race provided a great deal of the inspiration and guidance necessary for this project.

The Universal House of Justice and the friends in various departments of the Bahá'í World Centre responded quickly to my inquiries, and provided me with additional material for use in this compilation.

I am also most appreciative for the support and assistance of the Bahá'í National Education Task Force. I am particularly grateful for Leonard Smith's review of the manuscript, and his valuable suggestions.

Roger Dahl and Lewis Walker of National Bahá'í Archives were always available to provide research assistance, and enabled me to spend many exciting and fruitful days in search of new material. Roger and Lewis were interested, knowledgeable and responsive to all my questions and needs.

And finally, the faith, vision and enthusiasm of Charles Cornwell and Paul Lample of Palabra Publications were a source of great encouragement for me. I am grateful that they believed in the value of this work, and that they held the ideals and strength of commitment to transform the manuscript into a publication.

Our thanks also go to May Khadem Czerniejewski, M.D., an ophthalmologist, and Rick Czerniejewski, M.D., who lovingly prepared the beautiful description of the pupil of the eye that is included in this second edition.

Bonnie J. Taylor

The Pupil

The pupil of the eye is a portal which admits and regulates the flow of light to the retina. Without this passage, no images are perceived. At the retina, our consciousness is intimately in contact with physical reality, for the brain's cells themselves flow out to the retina to receive information through the illumination modulated by the pupil.

The pupil has the dual function of light gathering and modulation. Light, which unites all colors and is composed of all colors, illumines physical reality, but at the same time its intensity can destroy the delicate structures of the eye. When light levels are high, it constricts to protect the retina from intense and even damaging exposure. Since sight is often described as our most precious sensory ability, we can say that the pupil helps to protect this most precious gift. On the other hand, when there is very little light the pupil admits more light through dilating, thus permitting sight even in very dark places.

The black appearance of the pupil is deceptive. The pupil appears black only until the inside of the eye is illumined. Then it becomes radiant, filled with a warm, reddish-orange glow. With this reflection from the inside of the eye, the pupil itself becomes a source of illumination.

The most remarkable quality of the pupil is that despite its vital service, it is the embodiment of "the hollow reed from which the pith of self hath been blown," for it is the absence of physical structure that permits it to facilitate the harmonious functioning of all the other components of the eye that make sight possible.

Dr. Mary Khadem Czerniejewski & Dr. Richard Czerniejewski

ONE

People of African Descent

I. Qualities and Characteristics

> *Thou art like unto the pupil of the eye*
> *which is dark in color,*
> *yet it is the fount of light*
> *and the revealer of the contingent world.*
> 'Abdu'l-Bahá

1. Bahá'u'lláh . . . once compared the colored people† to the black pupil of the eye surrounded by the white. In this black pupil is seen the reflection of that which is before it, and through it the light of the spirit shineth forth.
   'Abdu'l-Bahá, in *The Advent of Divine Justice*, p. 31

2. O thou who hast an illumined heart! Thou art even as the pupil of the eye, the very wellspring of the light, for God's love hath cast its rays upon thine inmost being and thou hast turned thy face toward the Kingdom of thy Lord.
   Intense is the hatred, in America, between black and white, but my hope is that the power of the Kingdom will bind these two in friendship, and serve them as a healing balm.

---

† The Central Figures of the Bahá'í Faith, in their talks, tablets and letters, used terminology that was common and acceptable at the time.

Let them not look upon a man's color but upon his heart. If the heart be filled with light, that man is nigh unto the threshold of His Lord; but if not, that man is careless of His Lord, be he white or be he black.
  'Abdu'l-Bahá, *Selections from the Writings of 'Abdu'l-Bahá*, p. 113

3. O thou who art pure in heart, sanctified in spirit, peerless in character, beauteous in face! Thy photograph hath been received revealing thy physical frame in the utmost grace and the best appearance. Thou art dark in countenance and bright in character. Thou art like unto the pupil of the eye which is dark in color, yet it is the fount of light and the revealer of the contingent world.

I have not forgotten nor will I forget thee. I beseech God that He may graciously make thee the sign of His bounty amidst mankind, illumine thy face with the light of such blessings as are vouchsafed by the merciful Lord, single thee out for His love in this age which is distinguished among all the past ages and centuries.
  'Abdu'l-Bahá, *Selections from the Writings of 'Abdu'l-Bahá*, p. 114

4. Indeed, the hearts of the Africans are like unto a scroll which is free from any trace. It is possible for thee to write thereon any phrase, provided thou showest forth patience, and hast a heart as firm as a mighty mountain.
  'Abdu'l-Bahá, from a recently translated Tablet

5. The qualities of heart so richly possessed by the Negro are much needed in the world today—their great capacity for faith, their loyalty and devotion to their religion when once they believe, their purity of heart, God has richly endowed them, and their contribution to the Cause is much needed, especially as there is a lack of Negro Bahá'í teachers who can go out to their own people along with their white brothers and sisters, and convince them of the active universality of

our Faith. He will especially pray that you may confirm souls of capacity in this field.
> On behalf of Shoghi Effendi, *Lights of Guidance*, p. 403

6. The Negro Bahá'ís have much to contribute to the Cause. They are a deeply spiritual people with a great capacity for faith, and possess both patience and loyalty. He is very happy to see the way they are increasingly assuming their share of Bahá'í responsibility, and arising to dedicate themselves to the Cause of God in this day.
> On behalf of Shoghi Effendi, to individual believers, 3/17/43

7. He wishes you, in particular, to concentrate on teaching the Negro inhabitants . . . , and thus bring into the Cause this hitherto neglected, though highly promising and spiritually receptive, element of the population in the Southern States.
> On behalf of Shoghi Effendi, in *To Move the World*, pp. 255–56

8. I welcome with open arms the unexpectedly large number of the representatives of the pure-hearted and the spiritually receptive Negro race, so dearly loved by 'Abdu'l-Bahá, for whose conversion to His Father's Faith He so deeply yearned and whose interests He so ardently championed in the course of His memorable visit to the North American continent. I am reminded, on this historic occasion, of the significant words uttered by Bahá'u'lláh Himself, Who as attested by the Center of the Covenant, in His Writings, "compared the colored people to the black pupil of the eye," through which "the light of the spirit shineth forth." I feel particularly gratified by the substantial participation in this epoch-making conference of the members of the race dwelling in a continent which for the most part has retained its primitive simplicity and remained uncontaminated by the evils of a gross, a rampant and cancerous materialism undermining the fabric of human society alike in the East and in the West, eating into the vitals

of the conflicting peoples and races inhabiting the American, the European and the Asiatic continents, and alas threatening to engulf in one common catastrophic convulsion the generality of mankind.
Shoghi Effendi, *Messages to the Bahá'í World*, pp. 135-36

9. The spirit of the African believers is very touching, very noble, and indeed presents a challenge to their fellow-Bahá'ís all over the world. It seems that God has endowed these races, living in the so-called "dark" continent, with great spiritual faculties, and also with mental faculties, which, as they mature in the Faith, will contribute immensely to the whole, throughout the Bahá'í world.
Shoghi Effendi, to the Uganda Teaching Conference, 5/11/54

10. I cannot express to you in words how happy he is to welcome so many African coworkers into the glorious Cause of Bahá'u'lláh. He feels, from the letters they write him, the reports he receives, and above all, the quality of their deeds, that the people of Africa, especially those who become Bahá'ís, have wonderful characteristics which, when pooled with those of other nations and races, will greatly enrich our joint human heritage.
Shoghi Effendi, to an individual believer, 8/9/54

11. This vast, highly receptive, spiritually famished and long downtrodden Continent—the nest of the Negro race, constituting so large a proportion of the world's population—was first opened, in an hour of trial and adversity, in the lifetime of Bahá'u'lláh. . . .
Shoghi Effendi, to the Four African Conventions, 4/56

12. . . . many of the other countries [of Africa] represent a backward people, from the standpoint of modern civilization, but people much more receptive in heart and soul to the

Teachings of Bahá'u'lláh, much more sensitive to spiritual values, much readier indeed to embrace the Message of Bahá'u'lláh and arise in its service, as we have seen so wonderfully demonstrated during the last four years in the history of the Cause in Africa.
    Shoghi Effendi, to a National Spiritual Assembly, 7/2/56

13. Your cablegram giving the good news concerning the first South African Bahá'í who became confirmed in Pretoria July 12th was very encouraging indeed. Let us hope that this opens the door to the natives of South Africa, and will be the means of the spirit flowing in and giving immortal life to hundreds and thousands of these suppressed but pure-hearted peoples of South Africa.
    Shoghi Effendi, to a Hand of the Cause of God, 7/17/54

14. Surely they [the four Regional Conventions in Africa] were historic; for they marked the establishment of new pillars of the Universal House of Justice, in that newly awakening continent. Of greatest interest, is that most of the members of the Assemblies are of the black race, and represent such a large mass of people who have been for so long, mistreated and downtrodden. May this great event become the means of releasing new spiritual forces, which will bring these great peoples into their own, under the shade of the Blessed Tree of Bahá'u'lláh.
    Shoghi Effendi, to a Hand of the Cause of God, 6/11/56

15. I need not tell you that the work in Africa, and more particularly in Uganda, is very dear to his heart. The progress made there during the last year has borne him up and encouraged him greatly when he was often weighed down with work. He feels that this country and its peoples, in the very heart of Africa, are a most precious trust. Their receptivity to the Teachings, their great desire to serve their new

Faith, the number of them who have arisen to go out as pioneers, mark them as a people apart in the Bahá'í world, at least for the time being. May many others in neighboring countries prove as worthy, and follow their example.
    On behalf of Shoghi Effendi, *Unfolding Destiny*, p. 334

16. He was immensely pleased over the example shown by ... in withdrawing from political affiliation, and feels that some of the African friends are showing a most exemplary spirit of devotion and loyalty. He feels that a great potential strength lies in these new African believers.
    On behalf of Shoghi Effendi, *Unfolding Destiny*, p. 301

17. Recall with profound emotion message beloved Guardian occasion 1953 conference wherein he extolled pure hearted spiritually receptive indigenous people of Africa whom Bahá'u'lláh compared with the pupil of the eye, through which the light of the spirit shineth forth and for whose conversion both the Guardian and the Master before him yearned and labored....
    The Universal House of Justice, cable to the African Conference, 10/67, *Bahá'í News*, no. 441, 12/67, p. 28

18. Purity of heart, honesty of mind, sincerity of motive were characteristics deeply prized by Shoghi Effendi. These characteristics he felt were strongly represented in the so-called primitive peoples; they drew him to them and increased his conviction that the Cause of God has a tremendous future amongst the dark-skinned peoples of the world, and that they have great racial gifts of mind and heart to bring to the service of this Faith. It is significant to ponder that the first, the opening of this halfway point of the World Crusade was chosen by him for the heart of Africa, and that the last, the closing Conference, was set midway in the Pacific-Asian region. He did not thus honor the old world and the new. No, he chose the black people and the brown people for this

distinction. He visualized the African and the Pacific peoples vying with each other in the spread of the Faith. Each marked increase in membership in one region was relayed by him to the other, with the hope of stimulating a fresh burst of enthusiastic teaching efforts. Much of his joy, during the last years of his life, came from the news of the remarkable progress the Faith was making in these two areas.

> The Hands of the Cause in the Holy Land, to the Fifth Intercontinental Conference in Singapore, *Bahá'í News*, no. 333, 11/58, pp. 3–4

II. Individual Bahá'ís of African Descent

Louis G. Gregory

19. That pure soul has a heart like unto transparent water. He is like unto pure gold. This is why he is acceptable in any market and is current in every country.

> 'Abdu'l-Bahá, in *To Move the World*, p. 314

20. O Thou Wooer of Truth! Thy letter was received. Its contents indicated thy attainment to the Most Great Guidance. Thank God that thou hast attained to such a bounty, discovered the Path of the Kingdom and received the Glad-Tidings of the Universe of the Most High. This Divine Bestowal is conducive to the Everlasting Glory in both worlds. I hope that thou mayest become the Herald of the Kingdom, become the means whereby the white and colored peoples shall close their eyes to racial differences and behold the reality of humanity, and that is the universal unity which is the oneness of the kingdom of the human race, the basic harmony of the world and the appearance of the Bounty of the Almighty.

In brief, do not look upon thy weak body and thy limited capacity; look thou upon the Bounties and Providence of the Lord of the Kingdom, for His confirmation is great, and His Power unparalleled and incomparable. . . .
    'Abdu'l-Bahá, *The Bahá'í World*, vol. XII, pp. 667–68

21. O thou revered wife of his honor, Gregory!
Do thou consider what a bounty God hath bestowed upon thee in giving thee a husband as Mr. Gregory who is the essence of the love of God and is a symbol of guidance! How luminous is the face of this person! His character is (like unto) a rose-garden.
    'Abdu'l-Bahá, Tablet to Mrs. Louise Gregory

22. O ye two blessed souls!
Your letter was received. Praise be to God, that throughout these past years ye were engaged in the promulgation of the ideas of Universal Peace. At a time when misunderstanding among races was excessive, ye were engaged in bringing about full understanding. Ye have striven for the enlightenment of hearts by the light of Love and for the bestowal of sight and hearing upon the negligent; that the slumberer may awake and the ignorant be made heedful and aware.
I beg of God that in the pursuance of your benevolent purposes, ye may be assisted and confirmed.
Upon ye be greeting and praise!
    'Abdu'l-Bahá, to Mr. and Mrs. Louis Gregory, 12/30/18

23. My self-sacrificing brother in 'Abdu'l-Bahá!
Your splendid activities, your single-mindedness and devotion to the great work you are doing for the Cause is an inspiration to me in my task and a refreshment in the midst of my arduous duties. He who loved you, admired your capacity and was confident in your success is surely guiding every step you take and addresses you from on high "Well-

done, (Marhaba, Marhaba) my good and faithful friend!" What greater reward than the satisfaction and the good-pleasure of our dear Master which I am certain you have fully earned? I read the account of your travels with heartfelt joy and gratitude and I will continue to pray for you that you may be enabled to achieve still greater things for so glorious and mighty a Cause.
    Shoghi Effendi, to Louis Gregory, 4/4/25

24. My very dear and precious coworker:
    Your letter has infused strength and joy in my heart.... I have nothing but admiration and gratitude for the heroic constancy, mature wisdom, tireless energy, and shining love with which you are conducting your ever-expanding work of service to the Cause of Bahá'u'lláh. You hardly realize what a help you are to me in my arduous work. Your grateful brother....
    Shoghi Effendi, to Louis Gregory, in *To Move the World*, p. 177

25. The spirit which you have demonstrated, and which your welcome letter so powerfully reveals, is indeed worthy of the praise and admiration of the Supreme Concourse. The place you occupy in my heart, and the measure of admiration I cherish for the sublimity of your faith, I cannot describe. That you will visit Persia, as the worthy and first representative of your noble race in that historic land; that you will in the days to come supplement your great and memorable work in the states with further services in Europe, I feel assured and confident. In the meantime I wish you to concentrate, within the limits which your changed material position imposes, on the teaching work in America and particularly among the colored inhabitants. My prayers will accompany you, wherever you may be. With a heart filled with love and gratitude,
    Shoghi Effendi, to Louis Gregory, 10/20/32

26. Profoundly deplore grievous loss of dearly beloved, noble-minded, golden-hearted Louis Gregory, pride and example to the Negro adherents of the Faith. Keenly feel loss of one so loved, admired and trusted by 'Abdu'l-Bahá. Deserves rank of first Hand of the Cause of his race. Rising Bahá'í generation in African continent will glory in his memory and emulate his example. Advise hold memorial gathering in Temple in token recognition of his unique position, outstanding services.
    Shoghi Effendi, cable sent upon the passing of Louis Gregory, 8/6/51, *Citadel of Faith*, p. 163

Mrs. Pocohontas Pope

27. O handmaid of God!
Render thanks to the Lord that among that race† thou art the first believer,‡ that thou hast engaged in spreading sweet-

---

† 'Abdu'l-Bahá's reference to Mrs. Pope as being the first believer of "that race" may well relate to her being the first black person to accept the Faith in Washington, rather than in the United States. Alternatively, the Master may have been designating her with a special primacy, as He did with Thornton Chase. This could well be the subject of further research. (From the Research Department, Bahá'í World Centre, 1993, in "The Experience, Spiritual Qualities, Obligations and Destiny of Black People," p.1, footnote.)

‡ This Tablet was addressed to one Mrs. Pochahontas in Washington. According to Fádil Mázandaráni, the recipient of the Tablet was a black woman. See "Tárikh-i-Zuhúru'l-Haq", volume 8, part 2 p. 1209 (Ṭihrán: Bahá'í Publishing Trust, 132 B.E.) Additional information provided by the Archives of the National Spiritual Assembly of the United States indicates that Mr. Louis Gregory, in a history of the Washington D.C. Bahá'í community, mentions a black Bahá'í, Mrs. Pocohontas Pope, who is very likely the same person. Mrs. Pope learned of the Bahá'í Faith through Alma and Fanny Knobloch and Joseph and Pauline Hannen. There is, at present, no other information on Mrs. Pope. (From the Research Department of The Universal House of Justice, *Women*, footnote, p.3.)

scented breezes, and hast arisen to guide others. It is my hope that through the bounties and favors of the Abhá Beauty thy countenance may be illumined, thy disposition pleasing, and thy fragrance diffused, that thine eyes may be seeing, thine ears attentive, thy tongue eloquent, thy heart filled with supreme glad-tidings, and thy soul refreshed by divine fragrances, so that thou mayest arise among that race and occupy thyself with the edification of the people, and become filled with light. Although the pupil of the eye is black, it is the source of light. Thou shalt likewise be. The disposition should be bright not the appearance. Therefore, with supreme confidence and certitude, say: "O God! Make me a radiant light, a shining lamp, and a brilliant star, so that I may illumine the hearts with an effulgent ray from Thy Kingdom of Abhá...."
    'Abdu'l-Bahá, *Women*, p. 3

Isfandíyár

28. This is a beautiful assembly. I am very happy that white and black are together. This is the cause of my happiness, for you all are the servants of one God and, therefore, brothers, sisters, mothers and fathers. In the sight of God there is no distinction between whites and blacks; all are as one. Anyone whose heart is pure is dear to God—whether white or black, red or yellow. Among the animals colors exist. The doves are white, black, red, blue; but notwithstanding this diversity of color they flock together in unity, happiness and fellowship, making no distinction among themselves, for they are all doves. Man is intelligent and thoughtful, endowed with powers of mind. Why, then, should he be influenced by distinction of color or race, since all belong to one human family? There is no sheep which shuns another as if saying, "I am white, and you are black." They graze together in complete unity, live together in fellowship and happiness.

How then can man be limited and influenced by racial colors? The important thing is to realize that all are human, all are one progeny of Adam. Inasmuch as they are all one family, why should they be separated?

I had a servant who was black; his name was Isfandíyár. If a perfect man could be found in the world, that man was Isfandíyár. He was the essence of love, radiant with sanctity and perfection, luminous with light. Whenever I think of Isfandíyár, I am moved to tears, although he passed away fifty years ago. He was the faithful servant of Bahá'u'lláh and was entrusted with His secrets. For this reason the ×áh of Persia wanted him and inquired continually as to his whereabouts. Bahá'u'lláh was in prison, but the ×áh had commanded many persons to find Isfandíyár. Perhaps more than one hundred officers were appointed to search for him. If they had succeeded in catching him, they would not have killed him at once. They would have cut his flesh into pieces to force him to tell them the secrets of Bahá'u'lláh. But Isfandíyár with the utmost dignity used to walk in the streets and bazaars. One day he came to us. My mother, my sister and myself lived in a house near a corner. Because our enemies frequently injured us, we were intending to go to a place where they did not know us. I was a child at that time. At midnight Isfandíyár came in. My mother said, "O Isfandíyár, there are a hundred policemen seeking for you. If they catch you, they will not kill you at once but will torture you with fire. They will cut off your fingers. They will cut off your ears. They will put out your eyes to force you to tell them the secrets of Bahá'u'lláh. Go away! Do not stay here." He said, "I cannot go because I owe money in the street and in the stores. How can I go? They will say that the servant of Bahá'u'lláh has bought and consumed the goods and supplies of the storekeepers without paying for them. Unless I pay all these obligations, I cannot go. But if they take me, never mind. If they punish me, there is no harm in that. I must remain until I pay all I owe. Then I will go." For one month Isfandíyár went about in the streets and bazaars. He had things to sell, and from his earnings he gradually paid his creditors. In fact, they were not his debts but the debts of the court, for all our properties had been confiscated. Everything we had was taken away from us. The only things that remained were our debts. Isfandíyár paid them in full; not a single penny remained unpaid. Then he came to us, said good-bye and went away. Afterward Bahá'u'lláh was released from prison. We went to BaYdád, and Isfandíyár came there. He wanted to stay in the same home. Bahá'u'lláh, the Blessed Perfection, said to him, "When you fled away, there was a Persian minister who gave you shelter at a time when no one else could give you protection. Because he gave you shelter and protected you, you must be faithful to him. If he is satisfied to have you go, then come to us; but if he does not want you to go, do not leave him." His master said, "I do not want to be separated from Isfandíyár. Where can I find another like him, with such sincerity, such faithfulness, such character, such power? Where can I find one? O Isfandíyár! I am not willing that you should go, yet if you wish to go, let it be according to your own will." But because the Blessed Perfection had said, "You must be faithful," Isfandíyár stayed with his master until he died. He was a point of light. Although his color was black, yet his character was luminous; his mind was luminous; his face was luminous. Truly, he was a point of light.

'Abdu'l-Bahá, *The Promulgation of Universal Peace*, pp. 425–27

George Henderson

29. Thy letter that thou hast written in the beginning of December, 1920, has been received. Its contents contained very good news, indicating that his honor, Prof. George W.

Henderson, has established a Bahá'í College in one of the cities of the South; that now that college has developed, and the students are studying the Divine Teachings and also the necessary sciences and arts.

That revered professor has been and will always be favored. The meetings which are formed at that college are bestowed with an emanation from the meetings of the Supreme Concourse. Such are also the meetings for teaching the children. These meetings are spreading eternal graces and are supported by the breathings of the Holy Spirit. His honor, Prof. Henderson, has in reality arisen in the service of the Kingdom. The fruits of this service are eternal bounty and everlasting life. Through the graces of God do I cherish this hope, that he at every moment will receive a new confirmation.

'Abdu'l-Bahá, in *The Bahá'í World*, vol. VIII, p. 901

Robert Turner

30. ... Mrs. Hearst's butler, a Negro named Robert Turner, the first member of his race to embrace the Cause of Bahá'u'lláh in the West, had been transported by the influence exerted by 'Abdu'l-Bahá. ... Such was the tenacity of his faith that even the subsequent estrangement of his beloved mistress from the Cause she had spontaneously embraced failed to becloud its radiance, or to lessen the intensity of the emotions which the loving-kindness showered by 'Abdu'l-Bahá upon him had excited in his breast.

Shoghi Effendi, *God Passes By*, p. 259

Hand of the Cause of God Enoch Olinga

31. WITH GRIEF-STRICKEN HEARTS ANNOUNCE TRAGIC NEWS BRUTAL MURDER DEARLY LOVED

GREATLY ADMIRED HAND CAUSE GOD ENOCH OLINGA BY UNKNOWN GUNMEN COURTYARD HIS KAMPALA HOME. HIS WIFE ELIZABETH AND THREE OF HIS CHILDREN BADI, LENNIE AND TAHIRIH HAVE ALSO FALLEN INNOCENT VICTIMS THIS CRUEL ACT. MOTIVE ATTACK NOT YET ASCERTAINED. HIS RADIANT SPIRIT HIS UNWAVERING FAITH HIS ALL-EMBRACING LOVE HIS LEONINE AUDACITY IN THE TEACHING FIELD HIS TITLES KNIGHT BAHAULLAH FATHER VICTORIES CONFERRED BELOVED GUARDIAN ALL COMBINE DISTINGUISH HIM AS PREEMINENT MEMBER HIS RACE IN ANNALS FAITH AFRICAN CONTINENT. URGE FRIENDS EVERYWHERE HOLD MEMORIAL GATHERINGS BEFITTING TRIBUTE HIS IMPERISHABLE MEMORY. FERVENTLY PRAYING HOLY SHRINES PROGRESS HIS NOBLE SOUL AND SOULS FOUR MEMBERS HIS PRECIOUS FAMILY.

The Universal House of Justice, in *The Bahá'í World*, vol. XVIII, p. 634

Amoz Gibson

32. WITH SORROWFUL HEARTS LAMENT LOSS OUR DEARLY-LOVED BROTHER AMOZ GIBSON WHO PASSED AWAY AFTER PROLONGED ILLNESS. EXEMPLARY SELF-SACRIFICING PROMOTER FAITH ACHIEVED BRILLIANT UNBLEMISHED RECORD CONSTANT SERVICE FOUNDED ON ROCKLIKE STAUNCHNESS AND DEEP INSATIABLE LOVE FOR TEACHING WORK PARTICULARLY AMONG INDIAN AND BLACK MINORITIES WESTERN HEMISPHERE AND INDIGENOUS PEOPLES AFRICA. HIS NOTABLE WORK ADMINISTRATIVE FIELDS NORTH AMERICA CROWNED FINAL NINETEEN YEARS INCALCULABLE CONTRIBUTION DEVELOPMENT WORLD CENTRE

WORLD EMBRACING FAITH. PRAYING SHRINES BOUNTIFUL REWARD HIS NOBLE SOUL THROUGHOUT PROGRESS ABHA KINGDOM. EXPRESS LOVING SYMPATHY VALIANT BELOVED WIDOW PARTNER HIS SERVICES AND BEREAVED CHILDREN. ADVISE HOLD BEFITTING MEMORIAL GATHERINGS EVERYWHERE BAHAI WORLD AND COMMEMORATIVE SERVICES ALL MASHRIQUL ADHKARS.
>The Universal House of Justice, in *The Bahá'í World*, vol. XVIII, p. 669

Ellsworth Blackwell

33. GRIEVED PASSING VALIANT LONG TIME SERVANT CAUSE BAHAULLAH ELLSWORTH BLACKWELL STOP OUTSTANDING ENDEAVORS PIONEERING TEACHING ADMINISTRATIVE SERVICES MANY LANDS EVIDENCE HIS DEVOTION DEDICATION FAITH HE DEARLY LOVED STOP ASSURE WIFE FAMILY FRIENDS PRAYERS HOLY SHRINES PROGRESS HIS SOUL ABHA KINGDOM.
> The Universal House of Justice, in *The Bahá'í World*, vol. XVII, p. 453

Robert Hayden

34. GRIEVED PASSING ESTEEMED SERVANT CAUSE ROBERT HAYDEN. HIS NUMEROUS HONORS AND DISTINGUISHED CONTRIBUTION POETRY AMERICA ADDS LUSTRE ANNALS FAITH. KINDLY CONVEY TO FAMILY LOVING SYMPATHY ASSURANCE PRAYERS PROGRESS HIS SOUL.
> The Universal House of Justice, in *The Bahá'í World*, vol. XVIII, p. 717

Magdalene Carney

35. DEEPLY GRIEVED SUDDEN PASSING STALWART MAIDSERVANT BAHÁ'U'LLÁH MEMBER INTERNATIONAL TEACHING CENTER MAGDALENE M. CARNEY. HER WELL NIGH THREE DECADES UNBROKEN SERVICE CAUSE GOD EXERTED IMMENSE INFLUENCE TEACHING WORK SOUTHERN REGION UNITED STATES, INVOLVED THIRTEEN YEARS MEMBERSHIP NATIONAL SPIRITUAL ASSEMBLY THAT COUNTRY UNTIL HER APPOINTMENT IN 1983 TO INTERNATIONAL TEACHING CENTER. INDOMITABLE FAITH, UNSWERVING DEVOTION COVENANT, SELFLESS SPIRIT, OPEN CANDOR, WHOLEHEARTED COMMITMENT EDUCATION CHILDREN AND YOUTH ARE AMONG QUALITIES THAT WILL EVER BE ASSOCIATED WITH GOLDEN MEMORIES HER HIGHLY ACTIVE LIFE. ARDENTLY PRAYING HOLY THRESHOLD PROGRESS HER STERLING SOUL THROUGHOUT DIVINE WORLDS.

ADVISE HOLD MEMORIAL SERVICES HER HONOR ALL HOUSES WORSHIP AND IN BAHÁ'Í COMMUNITIES THROUGHOUT WORLD.

> The Universal House of Justice, in *The American Bahá'í*, 11/91, p. 1

TWO

Race

I. Origins of Racial Characteristics

> *All humanity are the children of God;*
> *they belong to the same family,*
> *to the same original race....*
> 'Abdu'l-Bahá

1. Now observe. The animal has no reasoning power and understanding, yet colors in animals do not give rise to differences. Why then should man, who is endowed with reason, create such differences? This is not at all worthy of him, especially as the white and black races have the same origin.
    'Abdu'l-Bahá, *The Promulgation of Universal Peace*, p. 45

2. Bahá'u'lláh especially emphasized international peace. He declared that all mankind is the one progeny of Adam and members of one great universal family. If the various races and distinct types of mankind had each proceeded from a different original paternity—in other words, if we had two or more Adams for our human fathers—there might be reasonable ground for difference and divergence in humanity today....
    'Abdu'l-Bahá, *The Promulgation of Universal Peace*, p. 354

3. Racial and national prejudices which separate mankind into groups and branches, likewise, have a false and unjusti-

fiable foundation, for all men are the children of Adam and essentially of one family.
    'Abdu'l-Bahá, *The Promulgation of Universal Peace*, p. 316

4. When we observe the human world, we find various collective expressions of unity therein. For instance, man is distinguished from the animal by his degree, or kingdom. This comprehensive distinction includes all the posterity of Adam and constitutes one great household or human family, which may be considered the fundamental or physical unity of mankind.
    'Abdu'l-Bahá, *The Promulgation of Universal Peace*, pp. 190–91

5. All humanity are the children of God; they belong to the same family, to the same original race. There can be no multiplicity of races, since all are the descendants of Adam.... We are of one physical race even as we are of one physical plan of material body; each endowed with two eyes, two ears, one head, two feet.
    'Abdu'l-Bahá, *'Abdu'l-Bahá in Canada*, p. 19

6. Bahá'u'lláh, addressing all humanity, said that Adam, the parent of mankind, may be likened to the tree of nativity upon which you are the leaves and blossoms. Inasmuch as your origin was one, you must now be united and agreed; you must consort with each other in joy and fragrance. He pronounced prejudice—whether religious, racial, patriotic, political—the destroyer of the body politic. He said that man must recognize the oneness of humanity, for all in origin belong to the same household, and all are servants of the same God.
    'Abdu'l-Bahá, *The Promulgation of Universal Peace*, p. 124

7. Indeed, the world of humanity is like one kindred and one family. Because of the climatic differences of the zones, through the passing of ages colors have become different. In

the torrid zone, on account of the intensity of the effect of the sun throughout the ages the black race appeared. In the frigid zone, on account of the severity of the cold and the ineffectiveness of the heat of the sun throughout the ages the white race appeared. In the temperate zone, the yellow, brown and red races came into existence. But in reality mankind is one race. Because it is of one race unquestionably there must be unity and harmony and no separation or discord.

Gracious God! The animal, notwithstanding that it is a captive of nature and nature completely dominateth it, attacheth no importance to color. For instance, thou dost behold that the black, white, yellow, blue and other colored pigeons are in utmost harmony with one another. They never give importance to color. Likewise sheep and the beasts, despite differences in color, are in utmost love and unity. It is strange that man hath made color a means of strife. Between the white and the black there is the utmost estrangement and discord.
    'Abdu'l-Bahá, *The Power of Unity*, p. 48

8. Now ponder this: Animals, despite the fact that they lack reason and understanding, do not make colors the cause of conflict. Why should man, who has reason, create conflict? This is wholly unworthy of him. Especially white and black are the descendants of the same Adam; they belong to one household. In origin they were one; they were the same color. Adam was of one color. Eve had one color. All humanity is descended from them. Therefore, in origin they are one. These colors developed later due to climates and regions; they have no significance whatsoever. Therefore, today I am very happy that white and black have gathered together in this meeting. I hope this coming together and harmony reaches such a degree that no distinctions shall remain between them, and they shall be together in the utmost harmony and love.
    'Abdu'l-Bahá, *The Promulgation of Universal Peace*, p. 45

II. Measurement of Human Intelligence, Capacity and Worth

> *There are no whites and blacks before God. . . .*
> *God does not look at colors; He looks at the hearts.*
> 'Abdu'l-Bahá

9. According to the words of the Old Testament God has said, "Let us make man in our image, after our likeness." This indicates that man is of the image and likeness of God—that is to say, the perfections of God, the divine virtues, are reflected or revealed in the human reality. Just as the light and effulgence of the sun when cast upon a polished mirror are reflected fully, gloriously, so, likewise, the qualities and attributes of Divinity are radiated from the depths of a pure human heart. This is an evidence that man is the most noble of God's creatures.

Each kingdom of creation is endowed with its necessary complement of attributes and powers. The mineral possesses inherent virtues of its own kingdom in the scale of existence. The vegetable possesses the qualities of the mineral plus an augmentative virtue, or power of growth. The animal is endowed with the virtues of both the mineral and vegetable plane plus the power of intellect. The human kingdom is replete with the perfections of all the kingdoms below it with the addition of powers peculiar to man alone. Man is, therefore, superior to all the creatures below him, the loftiest and most glorious being of creation. Man is the microcosm; and the infinite universe, the macrocosm. The mysteries of the greater world, or macrocosm, are expressed or revealed in the lesser world, the microcosm. The tree, so to speak, is the greater world, and the seed in its relation to the tree is the lesser world. But the whole of the great tree is potentially latent and hidden in the little seed. When this seed is planted and cultivated, the tree is revealed.

Likewise, the greater world, the macrocosm, is latent and miniatured in the lesser world, or microcosm, of man. This constitutes the universality or perfection of virtues potential in mankind. Therefore, it is said that man has been created in the image and likeness of God.

Let us now discover more specifically how he is the image and likeness of God and what is the standard or criterion by which he can be measured and estimated. This standard can be no other than the divine virtues which are revealed in him. Therefore, every man imbued with divine qualities, who reflects heavenly moralities and perfections, who is the expression of ideal and praiseworthy attributes, is, verily, in the image and likeness of God. If a man possesses wealth, can we call him an image and likeness of God? Or is human honor and notoriety the criterion of divine nearness? Can we apply the test of racial color and say that man of a certain hue—white, black, brown, yellow, red—is the true image of his Creator? We must conclude that color is not the standard and estimate of judgment and that it is of no importance, for color is accidental in nature. The spirit and intelligence of man is essential, and that is the manifestation of divine virtues, the merciful bestowals of God, the eternal life and baptism through the Holy Spirit. Therefore, be it known that color or race is of no importance. He who is the image and likeness of God, who is the manifestation of the bestowals of God, is acceptable at the threshold of God—whether his color be white, black or brown; it matters not. Man is not man simply because of bodily attributes. The standard of divine measure and judgment is his intelligence and spirit.

Therefore, let this be the only criterion and estimate, for this is the image and likeness of God. A man's heart may be pure and white though his outer skin be black; or his heart be dark and sinful though his racial color is white. The character and purity of the heart is of all importance. The heart illumined by the light of God is nearest and dearest to God, and

inasmuch as God has endowed man with such favor that he is called the image of God, this is truly a supreme perfection of attainment, a divine station which is not to be sacrificed by the mere accident of color.
>'Abdu'l-Bahá, Talk at Fourth Annual Conference of the NAACP, 4+30+12, *The Promulgation of Universal Peace*, p. 70

10. In the Kingdom of God no distinction is made as to the color of the skin, whether it be black or white; nay, rather the heart and soul are considered. If the spirit is pure, the face is illumined, although it be black. If the heart is stained, the face is dull and despondent, although it may be of the utmost beauty. The color of the pupils of the eye is black, yet they are the fountains of light.

Although white is conspicuous, yet seven colors are hidden and concealed therein. Therefore whiteness and blackness have no importance; nay, rather true judgment is based upon the soul and heart.
>'Abdu'l-Bahá, *The Power of Unity*, p. 6

11. There are no whites and blacks before God. All colors are one, and that is the color of servitude to God. Scent and color are not important. The heart is important. If the heart is pure, white or black or any color makes no difference. God does not look at colors; He looks at the hearts. He whose heart is pure is better. He whose character is better is more pleasing. He who turns more to the Abhá Kingdom is more advanced.
>'Abdu'l-Bahá, *The Promulgation of Universal Peace*, p. 44

12. This is a beautiful assembly. I am very happy that white and black are together. This is the cause of my happiness, for you all are the servants of one God and, therefore, brothers, sisters, mothers and fathers. In the sight of God there is no distinction between whites and blacks; all are as one. Anyone

whose heart is pure is dear to God—whether white or black, red or yellow.
  'Abdu'l-Bahá, *The Promulgation of Universal Peace*, p. 425

13. "God maketh no distinction between the white and the black. If the hearts are pure both are acceptable unto Him. God is no respecter of persons on account of either color or race. All colors are acceptable unto Him, be they white, black or yellow. Inasmuch as all were created in the image of God, we must bring ourselves to realize that all embody divine possibilities." "In the estimation of God, all men are equal. There is no distinction or preference for any soul, in the realm of His justice and equity." "God did not make these divisions; these divisions have had their origin in man himself. Therefore, as they are against the plan and purpose of God they are false and imaginary."
  'Abdu'l-Bahá, in *The Advent of Divine Justice*, p. 31

14. Intense is the hatred, in America, between black and white, but my hope is that the power of the Kingdom will bind these two in friendship, and serve them as a healing balm.
  Let them look not upon a man's color but upon his heart. If the heart be filled with light, that man is nigh unto the threshold of his Lord; but if not, that man is careless of his Lord, be he white or be he black.
  'Abdu'l-Bahá, *Selections from the Writings of 'Abdu'l-Bahá*, p. 113

15. God, the Almighty, has created all mankind from the dust of earth. He has fashioned them all from the same elements; they are descended from the same race and live upon the same globe. He has created them to dwell beneath the one heaven. As members of the human family and His children He has endowed them with equal susceptibilities. He main-

tains, protects and is kind to all. He has made no distinction in mercies and graces among His children.
    'Abdu'l-Bahá, *The Promulgation of Universal Peace*, p. 297

16. Then it is evident that excellence does not depend upon color. Character is the true criterion of humanity. Anyone who possesses a good character, who has faith in God and is firm, whose actions are good, whose speech is good—that one is accepted at the threshold of God no matter what color he may be. In short—praise be to God!—you are the servants of God. The love of Bahá'u'lláh is in your hearts. Your souls are rejoicing in the glad tidings of Bahá'u'lláh. My hope is that the white and the black will be united in perfect love and fellowship, with complete unity and brotherhood. Associate with each other, think of each other, and be like a rose garden.
    'Abdu'l-Bahá, *The Promulgation of Universal Peace*, pp. 427–28

III. The Intellect and Race

> *All the powers and attributes of man*
> *are human and hereditary in origin—*
> *outcomes of nature's processes—*
> *except the intellect, which is supernatural.*
>   'Abdu'l-Bahá

17. All blessings are divine in origin, but none can be compared with this power of intellectual investigation and research, which is an eternal gift producing fruits of unending delight. . . . Briefly, this is an eternal blessing and divine bestowal, the supreme gift of God to man. . . .

    How shall we utilize these gifts and expend these bounties? By directing our efforts toward the unification of the human race. We must use these powers in establishing the oneness of the world of humanity, appreciate these virtues by accomplishing the unity of whites and blacks, devote this

divine intelligence to the perfecting of amity and accord among all branches of the human family. . . .
    'Abdu'l-Bahá, *The Promulgation of Universal Peace*, pp. 50–51

18. The first condition of intelligence in the world of nature is the intelligence of the rational soul. In this intelligence and in this power all men are sharers. . . . This human rational soul is God's creation; it contains and excels other creatures. . . . All sciences, knowledge, arts, wonders, institutions, discoveries, and enterprises, come from the exercised intelligence of the rational soul.
    'Abdu'l-Bahá, *Some Answered Questions*, pp. 252–53

19. Now concerning mental faculties, they are in truth of the inherent properties of the soul, even as the radiation of light is the essential property of the sun. The rays of the sun are renewed but the sun itself is ever the same and unchanged. Consider how the human intellect develops and weakens, and may at times come to naught, whereas the soul changeth not. For the mind to manifest itself, the human body must be whole; and a sound mind cannot be but in a sound body, whereas the soul dependeth not upon the body. It is through the power of the soul that the mind comprehendeth, imagineth and exerteth its influence, whilst the soul is a power that is free. The mind comprehendeth the abstract by the aid of the concrete, but the soul hath limitless manifestations of its own. The mind is circumscribed, the soul limitless. It is by the aid of such senses as those of sight, hearing, taste, smell and touch, that the mind comprehendeth, whereas, the soul is free from all agencies."
    'Abdu'l-Bahá, *The Bahá'í Revelation*, p. 221

20. This intelligence of man is the intermediary between his body and his spirit.
    'Abdu'l-Bahá, *The Reality of Man*, p. 12

21. Now regarding the question whether the faculties of the mind and the human soul are one and the same. These faculties are but the inherent properties of the soul, such as the power of imagination, of thought, of understanding; powers that are the essential requisites of the reality of man, even as the solar ray is the inherent property of the sun. The temple of man is like unto a mirror, his soul is as the sun, and his mental faculties even as the rays that emanate from that source of light.
  'Abdu'l-Bahá, *The Bahá'í Revelation*, pp. 229–30

22. The human spirit which distinguishes man from the animal is the rational soul; and these two names—the human spirit and the rational soul—designate one thing. This spirit, which in the terminology of the philosophers is the rational soul, embraces all beings, and as far as human ability permits discovers the realities of things and becomes cognizant of their peculiarities and effects, and of the qualities and properties of beings. . . .

But the mind is the power of the human spirit. Spirit is the lamp; mind is the light which shines from the lamp. Spirit is the tree, and the mind is the fruit. Mind is the perfection of the spirit, and is its essential quality, as the sun's rays are the essential necessity of the sun.
  'Abdu'l-Bahá, *Bahá'í World Faith*, pp. 316–17

23. Likewise the Holy Spirit is the very cause of the life of man; without the Holy Spirit he would have no intellect, he would be unable to acquire his scientific knowledge by which his great influence over the rest of creation is gained. . . .

  The Holy Spirit it is which, through the mediation of the prophets of God, teaches spiritual virtues to man and enables him to attain eternal life.
  'Abdu'l-Bahá, *The Reality of Man*, p. 46

24. All the powers and attributes of man are human and hereditary in origin—outcomes of nature's processes—except the intellect, which is supernatural.
    'Abdu'l-Bahá, *The Promulgation of Universal Peace*, p. 49

25. The Manifestations of God are likewise in agreement with the view that education exerteth the strongest possible influence on humankind. They affirm, however, that differences in the level of intelligence are innate; and this fact is obvious, and not worth debating. For we see that children of the same age, the same country, the same race, indeed of the same family, and trained by the same individual, still are different as to the degree of their comprehension and intelligence. One will make rapid progress, one will receive instruction only gradually, one will remain at the lowest stage of all.... That is to say, education cannot alter the inner essence of a man, but it doth exert tremendous influence, and with this power it can bring forth from the individual whatever perfections and capacities are deposited within him.... A grain of wheat, when cultivated by the farmer, will yield a whole harvest, and a seed, through the gardener's care, will grow into a great tree. Thanks to a teacher's loving efforts, the children of the primary school may reach the highest levels of achievement; indeed, his benefactions may lift some child of small account to an exalted throne. Thus is it clearly demonstrated that by their essential nature, minds vary as to their capacity, while education also playeth a great role and exerteth a powerful effect on their development.
    'Abdu'l-Bahá, *Selections from the Writings of 'Abdu'l-Bahá*, pp. 131–32

Three

Bahá'u'lláh's Principle of the Oneness of Mankind

I. The Fundamental Principle of the Bahá'í Faith

O Children of Men!
Know ye not why We created you all from the same dust?
That no one should exalt himself over the other.
Bahá'u'lláh

1. The utterance of God is a lamp, whose light are these words: Ye are the fruits of one tree, and the leaves of one branch. Deal ye one with another with the utmost love and harmony, with friendliness and fellowship. He Who is the Day-Star of Truth beareth Me witness! So powerful is the light of unity that it can illuminate the whole earth. The One true God, He Who knoweth all things, Himself testifieth to the truth of these words.
   Bahá'u'lláh, *Epistle to the Son of the Wolf,* p. 14

2. The Great Being saith: O ye children of men! The fundamental purpose animating the Faith of God and His Religion is to safeguard the interests and promote the unity of the human race, and to foster the spirit of love and fellowship amongst men.
   Bahá'u'lláh, *Gleanings,* p. 215

3. That which the Lord hath ordained as the sovereign remedy and mightiest instrument for the healing of all the world is the union of all its peoples in one universal Cause, one common Faith.
    Bahá'u'lláh, *Gleanings*, p. 255

4. O Children of Men! Know ye not why We created you all from the same dust? That no one should exalt himself over the other. Ponder at all times in your hearts how ye were created. Since We have created you all from one same substance it is incumbent on you to be even as one soul, to walk with the same feet, eat with the same mouth and dwell in the same land, that from your inmost being, by your deeds and actions, the signs of oneness and the essence of detachment may be made manifest. Such is My counsel to you, O concourse of light! Heed ye this counsel that ye may obtain the fruit of holiness from the tree of wondrous glory.
    Bahá'u'lláh, *The Hidden Words*, Arabic no. 68

5. He Who is your Lord, the All-Merciful, cherisheth in His heart the desire of beholding the entire human race as one soul and one body.
    Bahá'u'lláh, *Gleanings*, p. 214

6. If any differences arise amongst you, behold Me standing before your face, and overlook the faults of one another for My name's sake and as a token of your love for My manifest and resplendent Cause. We love to see you at all times consorting in amity and concord within the paradise of My good-pleasure, and to inhale from your acts the fragrance of friendliness and unity, of loving-kindness and fellowship. Thus counselleth you the All-Knowing, the Faithful. We shall always be with you; if We inhale the perfume of your fellowship, Our heart will assuredly rejoice, for naught else can satisfy Us.
    Bahá'u'lláh, *Gleanings*, pp. 315–16

7. O contending peoples and kindreds of the earth! Set your faces towards unity, and let the radiance of its light shine upon you. Gather ye together, and for the sake of God resolve to root out whatever is the source of contention amongst you. Then will the effulgence of the world's great Luminary envelop the whole earth, and its inhabitants become the citizens of one city, and the occupants of one and the same throne.
    Bahá'u'lláh, *Gleanings*, p. 217

8. That one indeed is a man who, today, dedicateth himself to the service of the entire human race. The Great Being saith: Blessed and happy is he that ariseth to promote the best interests of the peoples and kindreds of the earth. In another passage He hath proclaimed: It is not for him to pride himself who loveth his own country, but rather for him who loveth the whole world. The earth is but one country; and mankind its citizens.
    Bahá'u'lláh, *Tablets of Bahá'u'lláh*, p. 167

9. And among the realms of unity is the unity of rank and station. It redoundeth to the exaltation of the Cause, glorifying it among all peoples. Ever since the seeking of preference and distinction came into play, the world hath been laid waste. It hath become desolate. Those who have quaffed from the ocean of divine utterance and fixed their gaze upon the Realm of Glory should regard themselves as being on the same level as the others and in the same station. Were this matter to be definitely established and conclusively demonstrated through the power and might of God, the world would become as the Abhá Paradise.

    Indeed, man is noble, inasmuch as each one is a repository of the sign of God. Nevertheless, to regard oneself as superior in knowledge, learning or virtue, or to exalt oneself or seek preference, is a grievous transgression. Great is the

blessedness of those who are adorned with the ornament of this unity and have been graciously confirmed by God.
> Bahá'u'lláh, in a letter from The Universal House of Justice to all National Spiritual Assemblies, 3/27/78

10. Regard ye the world as a man's body, which is afflicted with divers ailments, and the recovery of which dependeth upon the harmonizing of all its component elements.
> Bahá'u'lláh, *Epistle to the Son of the Wolf*, p. 55

11. Become as true brethren in the one and indivisible religion of God, free from distinction, for verily God desireth that your hearts should become mirrors unto your brethren in the Faith, so that ye find yourselves reflected in them, and they in you.
> The Báb, *Selections from the Writings of the Báb*, p. 56

12. Today the one overriding need is unity and harmony among the beloved of the Lord, for they should have among them but one heart and soul and should, so far as in them lieth, unitedly withstand the hostility of all the peoples of the world; they must bring to an end the benighted prejudices of all nations and religions and must make known to every member of the human race that all are the leaves of one branch, the fruits of one bough.
> 'Abdu'l-Bahá, *Selections from the Writings of 'Abdu'l-Bahá*, p. 277

13. Another unity is the spiritual unity which emanates from the breaths of the Holy Spirit. This is greater than the unity of mankind. Human unity or solidarity may be likened to the body, whereas unity from the breaths of the Holy Spirit is the spirit animating the body. This is perfect unity. It creates such a condition in mankind that each one will make sacrifices for the other, and the utmost desire will be to forfeit life and all that pertains to it in behalf of another's good. This is the unity which existed among the disciples of Jesus Christ and bound

together the Prophets and holy Souls of the past. It is the unity which through the influence of the divine spirit is permeating the Bahá'ís so that each offers his life for the other and strives with all sincerity to attain his good pleasure. This is the unity which caused twenty thousand people in Persia to give their lives in love and devotion to it. It made the Báb the target of a thousand arrows and caused Bahá'u'lláh to suffer exile and imprisonment forty years. This unity is the very spirit of the body of the world. It is impossible for the body of the world to become quickened with life without its vivification.

'Abdu'l-Bahá, *The Promulgation of Universal Peace*, pp. 191–92

14. As preordained by the Fountainhead of Creation, the temple of the world hath been fashioned after the image and likeness of the human body. In fact each mirroreth forth the image of the other, wert thou but to observe with discerning eyes. By this is meant that even as the human body in this world which is outwardly composed of different limbs and organs, is in reality a closely integrated, coherent entity, similarly the structure of the physical world is like unto a single being whose limbs and members are inseparably linked together.

Were one to observe with an eye that discovereth the realities of all things, it would become clear that the greatest relationship that bindeth the world of being together lieth in the range of created things themselves, and that cooperation, mutual aid and reciprocity are essential characteristics in the unified body of the world of being, inasmuch as all created things are closely related together and each is influenced by the other or deriveth benefit therefrom, either directly or indirectly.

Consider for instance how one group of created things constituteth the vegetable kingdom, and another the animal kingdom. Each of these two maketh use of certain elements in the air on which its own life dependeth, while each increaseth the quantity of such elements as are essential for the life of the other. In other words, the growth and development of the vegetable world is impossible without the existence of the animal kingdom, and the maintenance of animal life is inconceivable without the cooperation of the vegetable kingdom. Of like kind are the relationships that exist among all created things. Hence it was stated that cooperation and reciprocity are essential properties which are inherent in the unified system of the world of existence, and without which the entire creation would be reduced to nothingness.

In surveying the vast range of creation thou shalt perceive that the higher a kingdom of created things is on the arc of ascent, the more conspicuous are the signs and evidences of the truth that cooperation and reciprocity at the level of a higher order are greater than those that exist at the level of a lower order. For example the evident signs of this fundamental reality are more discernible in the vegetable kingdom than in the mineral, and still more manifest in the animal world than in the vegetable.

And thus when contemplating the human world thou beholdest this wondrous phenomenon shining resplendent from all sides with the utmost perfection, inasmuch as in this station acts of cooperation, mutual assistance and reciprocity are not confined to the body and to things that pertain to the material world, but for all conditions, whether physical or spiritual, such as those related to minds, thoughts, opinions, manners, customs, attitudes, understandings, feelings or other human susceptibilities. In all these thou shouldst find these binding relationships securely established. The more this inter-relationship is strengthened and expanded, the more will human society advance in progress and prosperity. Indeed without these vital ties it would be wholly impossible for the world of humanity to attain true felicity and success.

Now consider, if among the people who are merely the manifestations of the world of being this significant matter is of such importance, how much greater must be the spirit of cooperation and mutual assistance among those who are the essences of the world of creation, who have sought the sheltering shadow of the heavenly Tree, and are favored by the manifestations of divine grace; and how the evidences of this spirit should, through their earnest endeavor, their fellowship and concord, become manifest in every sphere of their inner and outer lives, in the realm of the spirit and divine mysteries and in all things related to this world and the next. Thus there can be no doubt that they must be willing even to offer up their lives for each other.
    'Abdu'l-Bahá, *Ḥuqúqu'lláh*, pp. 21–22

15. Reflect ye as to other than human forms of life and be ye admonished thereby: those clouds that drift apart cannot produce the bounty of the rain, and are soon lost; a flock of sheep, once scattered, falleth prey to the wolf, and birds that fly alone will be caught fast in the claws of the hawk. What greater demonstration could there be that unity leadeth to flourishing life, while dissension and withdrawing from others, will lead only to misery; for these are the sure ways to bitter disappointment and ruin.
    'Abdu'l-Bahá, *Selections from the Writings of 'Abdu'l-Bahá*, p. 278

16. We belong to an organic unit and when one part of the organism suffers all the rest of the body will feel its consequence. This is in fact the reason why Bahá'u'lláh calls our attention to the unity of mankind.
    Shoghi Effendi, *Lights of Guidance*, p. 92

17. . . . the object of life to a Bahá'í is to promote the oneness of mankind. The whole object of our lives is bound up with the lives of all human beings; not a personal salvation we are seeking, but a universal one. . . . Our aim is to produce a world

civilization which will in turn react on the character of the individual.
> Shoghi Effendi, quoted by Rúḥíyyih Khánum in *Bahá'í News*, no. 231, 5/50, p. 6

18. Let there be no mistake. The principle of the Oneness of Mankind—the pivot round which all the teachings of Bahá'u'lláh revolve—is no mere outburst of ignorant emotionalism or an expression of vague and pious hope. Its appeal is not to be merely identified with a reawakening of the spirit of brotherhood and good-will among men, nor does it aim solely at the fostering of harmonious cooperation among individual peoples and nations. Its implications are deeper, its claims greater than any which the Prophets of old were allowed to advance. Its message is applicable not only to the individual, but concerns itself primarily with the nature of those essential relationships that must bind all the states and nations as members of one human family. It does not constitute merely the enunciation of an ideal, but stands inseparably associated with an institution adequate to embody its truth, demonstrate its validity, and perpetuate its influence. It implies an organic change in the structure of present-day society, a change such as the world has not yet experienced. It constitutes a challenge, at once bold and universal, to outworn shibboleths of national creeds—creeds that have had their day and which must, in the ordinary course of events as shaped and controlled by Providence, give way to a new gospel, fundamentally different from, and infinitely superior to, what the world has already conceived. It calls for no less than the reconstruction and the demilitarization of the whole civilized world—a world organically unified in all the essential aspects of its life, its political machinery, its spiritual aspiration, its trade and finance, its script and language, and yet infinite in the diversity of the national characteristics of its federated units.

It represents the consummation of human evolution—an evolution that has had its earliest beginnings in the birth of family life, its subsequent development in the achievement of tribal solidarity, leading in turn to the constitution of the city-state, and expanding later into the institution of independent and sovereign nations.

The principle of the Oneness of Mankind, as proclaimed by Bahá'u'lláh, carries with it no more and no less than a solemn assertion that attainment to this final stage in this stupendous evolution is not only necessary but inevitable, that its realization is fast approaching, and that nothing short of a power that is born of God can succeed in establishing it.

So marvellous a conception finds its earliest manifestations in the efforts consciously exerted and the modest beginnings already achieved by the declared adherents of the Faith of Bahá'u'lláh who, conscious of the sublimity of their calling and initiated into the ennobling principles of His Administration, are forging ahead to establish His Kingdom on this earth. It has its indirect manifestations in the gradual diffusion of the spirit of world solidarity which is spontaneously arising out of the welter of a disorganized society.

Shoghi Effendi, *The World Order of Bahá'u'lláh*, pp. 42–43

19. The Faith of Bahá'u'lláh has assimilated, by virtue of its creative, its regulative and ennobling energies, the varied races, nationalities, creeds and classes that have sought its shadow, and have pledged unswerving fealty to its cause. It has changed the hearts of its adherents, burned away their prejudices, stilled their passions, exalted their conceptions, ennobled their motives, coordinated their efforts, and transformed their outlook. While preserving their patriotism and safeguarding their lesser loyalties, it has made them lovers of mankind, and the determined upholders of its best and truest interests. While maintaining intact their belief in the Divine origin of their respective religions, it has enabled them to

visualize the underlying purpose of these religions, to discover their merits, to recognize their sequence, their interdependence, their wholeness and unity, and to acknowledge the bond that vitally links them to itself. This universal, this transcending love which the followers of the Bahá'í Faith feel for their fellow-men, of whatever race, creed, class or nation, is neither mysterious nor can it be said to have been artificially stimulated. It is both spontaneous and genuine. They whose hearts are warmed by the energizing influence of God's creative love cherish His creatures for His sake, and recognize in every human face a sign of His reflected glory.

Of such men and women it may be truly said that to them "every foreign land is a fatherland, and every fatherland a foreign land."
    Shoghi Effendi, *The World Order of Bahá'u'lláh*, pp. 197–98

20. In every Dispensation the light of Divine Guidance has been focussed upon one central theme.... In this wondrous Revelation, this glorious century, the foundation of the Faith of God, and the distinguishing feature of His Law, is the consciousness of the oneness of mankind.
    'Abdu'l-Bahá, in *The Promised Day Is Come*, pp. 123–24

21. When Bahá'u'lláh proclaimed His Message to the world in the nineteenth century He made it abundantly clear that the first step essential for the peace and progress of mankind was its unification. As He says, "The well-being of mankind, its peace and security are unattainable unless and until its unity is firmly established."... To this day, however, you will find most people take the opposite point of view: they look upon unity as an ultimate, almost unattainable goal and concentrate first on remedying all the other ills of mankind. If they did but know it, these other ills are but various symptoms and side effects of the basic disease—disunity.
    The Universal House of Justice, *Wellspring of Guidance*, p. 131

II. Eliminating Prejudices: Prerequisite to Unity and Peace

> *For the accomplishment of unity*
> *between the colored and white*
> *will be an assurance of the world's peace.*
> 'Abdu'l-Bahá

22. That all nations should become one in faith and all men as brothers; that the bonds of affection and unity between the sons of men should be strengthened; that diversity of religion should cease, and differences of race be annulled—what harm is there in this? . . . Yet so it shall be; these fruitless strifes, these ruinous wars shall pass away, and the "Most Great Peace" shall come. . . . These strifes and this bloodshed and discord must cease, and all men be as one kindred and one family. . . . Let not a man glory in this, that he loves his country; let him rather glory in this, that he loves his kind. . . .

Bahá'u'lláh, in *Bahá'u'lláh and the New Era*, p. 40

23. With reference to your question as to the meaning of the passage, "he who loves his kind"; the statement of Bahá'u'lláh does not refer to any special race or class of people. Rather it includes the entire human race, irrespective of any class, creed or color. The Message of Bahá'u'lláh is not a particularistic appeal to a group of people. It is a Universal Message, an all-inclusive appeal. His principle of the Oneness of Mankind is worldwide in its spirit, in its application, and covers the entire field of human relationships.

It is most essential that the believers should be quite clear on this point, as the principle of the oneness of humanity is the cornerstone of all the Teachings of Bahá'u'lláh, and should be presented as such, without the least hesitation, by the friends.

Shoghi Effendi, to an individual believer, 3/11/37

24. And among the teachings of Bahá'u'lláh is that religious, racial, political, economic and patriotic prejudices destroy the edifice of humanity. As long as these prejudices prevail, the world of humanity will have no rest. For a period of six thousand years history informs us about the world of humanity. During these six thousand years the world of humanity has not been free from war, strife, murder and bloodthirstiness. In every period war has been waged in one country or another, and that war was due to either religious prejudice, racial prejudice, political prejudice or patriotic prejudice. It has, therefore, been ascertained and proved that all prejudices are destructive of the human edifice. As long as these prejudices persist, the struggle for existence must remain dominant, and bloodthirstiness and rapacity continue.
    'Abdu'l-Bahá, *Foundations of World Unity*, p. 29

25. The earth is one earth, and the same atmosphere surrounds it. No difference or preference has been made by God for its human inhabitants; but man has laid the foundation of prejudice, hatred and discord with his fellowman by considering nationalities separate in importance and races different in rights and privileges.
    'Abdu'l-Bahá, *The Promulgation of Universal Peace*, p. 232

26. And the breeding-ground of all these tragedies [wars] is prejudice: prejudice of race and nation, of religion, of political opinion; and the root cause of prejudice is blind imitation of the past—imitation in religion, in racial attitudes, in national bias, in politics. So long as this aping of the past persisteth, just so long will the foundations of the social order be blown to the four winds, just so long will humanity be continually exposed to direst peril.
    'Abdu'l-Bahá, *Selections from the Writings of 'Abdu'l-Bahá*, p. 247

27. Rivalry between the different races of mankind was first caused by the struggle for existence among the wild animals. This struggle is no longer necessary: nay, rather! interdependence and cooperation are seen to produce the highest welfare in nations. The struggle that now continues is caused by prejudice and bigotry.
    'Abdu'l-Bahá, *Star of the West*, vol. II, no. 9, p. 5

28. God has created His servants in order that they may love and associate with each other. He has revealed the glorious splendor of His sun of love in the world of humanity. The cause of the creation of the phenomenal world is love. All the Prophets have promulgated the law of love. Man has opposed the will of God and acted in opposition to the plan of God. Therefore, from the beginning of history to the present time the world of humanity has had no lasting rest; warfare and strife have continuously prevailed, and hearts have manifested hatred toward each other. The cause of bloodshed and battle, strife and hatred throughout the past has been either religious, racial, patriotic or political prejudice. Therefore, the world of humanity has ever been in torment.
    'Abdu'l-Bahá, *The Promulgation of Universal Peace*, pp. 297–98

29. Love is unlimited, boundless, infinite! Material things are limited, circumscribed, finite. You cannot adequately express infinite love by limited means.

    The perfect love needs an unselfish instrument, absolutely freed from fetters of every kind. The love of family is limited; the tie of blood relationship is not the strongest bond. Frequently members of the same family disagree, and even hate each other.

    Patriotic love is finite; the love of one's country causing hatred of all others, is not perfect love! Compatriots also are not free from quarrels amongst themselves.

The love of race is limited; there is some union here, but that is insufficient. Love must be free from boundaries!

To love our own race may mean hatred of all others, and even people of the same race often dislike each other.

Political love also is much bound up with hatred of one party for another; this love is very limited and uncertain.

The love of community of interest in service is likewise fluctuating; frequently competitions arise, which lead to jealousy, and at length hatred replaces love. . . .

All these ties of love are imperfect. It is clear that limited material ties are insufficient to adequately express the universal love.

The great unselfish love for humanity is bounded by none of these imperfect, semi-selfish bonds; this is the one perfect love, possible to all mankind, and can only be achieved by the power of the Divine Spirit. No worldly power can accomplish the universal love.
'Abdu'l-Bahá, *Paris Talks*, pp. 36–37

30. In the human kingdom itself there are points of contact, properties common to all mankind; likewise, there are points of distinction which separate race from race, individual from individual. If the points of contact, which are the common properties of humanity, overcome the peculiar points of distinction, unity is assured. On the other hand, if the points of differentiation overcome the points of agreement, disunion and weakness result. One of the important questions which affect the unity and the solidarity of mankind is the fellowship and equality of the white and colored races. Between these two races certain points of agreement and points of distinction exist which warrant just and mutual consideration. The points of contact are many; for in the material or physical plane of being, both are constituted alike and exist under the same law of growth and bodily development. Furthermore, both live and move in the plane of the

senses and are endowed with human intelligence. There are many other mutual qualifications. In this country, the United States of America, patriotism is common to both races; all have equal rights to citizenship, speak one language, receive the blessings of the same civilization, and follow the precepts of the same religion. In fact numerous points of partnership and agreement exist between the two races; whereas the one point of distinction is that of color. Shall this, the least of all distinctions, be allowed to separate you as races and individuals? In physical bodies, in the law of growth, in sense endowment, intelligence, patriotism, language, citizenship, civilization and religion you are one and the same. A single point of distinction exists—that of racial color. God is not pleased with—neither should any reasonable or intelligent man be willing to recognize—inequality in the races because of this distinction.
 'Abdu'l-Bahá, *The Promulgation of Universal Peace*, pp. 67–68

31. If five people meet together to seek for truth, they must begin by cutting themselves free from all their own special conditions and renouncing all preconceived ideas. In order to find truth we must give up our prejudices, our own small trivial notions; an open receptive mind is essential. If our chalice is full of self, there is no room in it for the water of life. The fact that we imagine ourselves to be right and everybody else wrong is the greatest of all obstacles in the path towards unity, and unity is necessary if we would reach truth, for truth is one.
 'Abdu'l-Bahá, *Paris Talks*, p. 136

32. When the racial elements of the American nation unite in actual fellowship and accord, the lights of the oneness of humanity will shine, the day of eternal glory and bliss will dawn, the spirit of God encompass, and the divine favors descend. Under the leadership and training of God, the real

Shepherd, all will be protected and preserved. He will lead them in green pastures of happiness and sustenance, and they will attain to the real goal of existence. This is the blessing and benefit of unity; this is the outcome of love. This is the sign of the Most Great Peace; this is the star of the oneness of the human world. Consider how blessed this condition will be. I pray for you and ask the confirmation and assistance of God in your behalf.
    'Abdu'l-Bahá, *The Promulgation of Universal Peace*, p. 57

33. The thoughts of man shall take such upward flight that former accomplishments shall appear as the play of children;—for the ideas and beliefs of the past and the prejudices regarding race and religion have ever been lowering and destructive to human evolution.
    'Abdu'l-Bahá, *Foundations of World Unity*, p. 21

34. The theories and policies, so unsound, so pernicious, which deify the state and exalt the nation above mankind, which seek to subordinate the sister races of the world to one single race, which discriminate between the black and the white, and which tolerate the dominance of one privileged class over all others—these are the dark, the false, and crooked doctrines for which any man or people who believes in them, or acts upon them, must, sooner or later, incur the wrath and chastisement of God.
    Shoghi Effendi, *The Promised Day Is Come*, p. 118

35. Regarding the solution to the racial problem; the believers should of course realize that the principle of the oneness of mankind which is the cornerstone of the message of Bahá'u'lláh is wholly incompatible with all forms of racial prejudice. Loyalty to this foundation principle of the Faith is the paramount duty of every believer and should be therefore wholehearted and unqualified. For a Bahá'í, racial

prejudice, in all its forms, is simply a negation of faith, an attitude wholly incompatible with the very spirit and actual teachings of the Cause.

On behalf of Shoghi Effendi, *Bahá'í News*, no. 105, 2/37, p. 1

36. The teachings of Bahá'u'lláh will establish a new way of life for humanity. Those who are Bahá'ís must endeavor to establish this way of life just as rapidly as possible. Now that the hour has arrived when the Bahá'í Faith is gaining prominence, and is being reviewed by so many peoples, it is necessary that the adherents of the Faith should live up to the high ideals of the Faith in every way. In this way they can demonstrate that the Bahá'í Faith does create a new way of life, which brings to the individual a complete association with the Will of God, and thus the establishment of a peaceful and universal society. Divisional attachments are of men, while universal service is of God.

The Guardian is now anxious that all the friends achieve a universal consciousness and universal way of life.

On behalf of Shoghi Effendi, 11/20/55

37. The attitude of the Cause towards the problem of race, be it in America or elsewhere, has been repeatedly clarified by the Guardian. To the faithful followers of Bahá'u'lláh who fully grasp the essential implications of the principle of the oneness of mankind so much emphasized in His teachings, racial prejudice, in all its forms, is simply a negation of faith, a repudiation of the belief in the brotherhood of man which is, beyond doubt, the cornerstone of the Religion of God. Loyalty to this basic principle should, therefore, be wholehearted and unqualified.

On behalf of Shoghi Effendi, to an individual believer, 11/11/36

38. World order can be founded only on an unshakable consciousness of the oneness of mankind, a spiritual truth

which all the human sciences confirm. Anthropology, physiology, psychology, recognize only one human species, albeit infinitely varied in the secondary aspects of life. Recognition of this truth requires abandonment of prejudice—prejudice of every kind—race, class, color, creed, nation, sex, degree of material civilization, everything which enables people to consider themselves superior to others.
>   The Universal House of Justice, *The Promise of World Peace*, pp. 28–29

39. Racism, one of the most baneful and persistent evils, is a major barrier to peace. Its practice perpetrates too outrageous a violation of the dignity of human beings to be countenanced under any pretext. Racism retards the unfoldment of the boundless potentialities of its victims, corrupts its perpetrators, and blights human progress. Recognition of the oneness of mankind, implemented by appropriate legal measures, must be universally upheld if this problem is to be overcome.
>   The Universal House of Justice, *The Promise of World Peace*, p. 25

III. The Danger of Prejudice and Disunity

> *This question of the union of the white and the black*
> *is very important, for if it is not realized,*
> *erelong great difficulties will arise,*
> *and harmful results will follow.*
> 'Abdu'l-Bahá

40. As with the whole, so with the parts; whether a flower or a human body, when the attracting principle is withdrawn from it, the flower or the man dies. It is therefore clear that attraction, harmony, unity and love, are the cause of life, whereas repulsion, discord, hatred and separation bring death.

We have seen that whatever brings division into the world of existence causes death. Likewise in the world of the spirit does the same law operate.
'Abdu'l-Bahá, *Paris Talks*, p. 139

41. To bring the white and the black together is considered impossible and unfeasible, but the breaths of the Holy Spirit will bring about this union.

... the enmity and hatred which exist between the white and the black races is very dangerous and there is no doubt that it will end in bloodshed unless the influence of the Word of God, the breaths of the Holy Spirit and the teachings of Bahá'u'lláh are diffused amongst them and harmony is established between the two races.

They must destroy the foundation of enmity and rancor and lay the basis of love and affinity. The power of the Teachings of Bahá'u'lláh will remove this danger from America.
'Abdu'l-Bahá, *The Power of Unity*, p. 31

42. The glad tidings of the progress of the Cause of God in that country is the cause of happiness. I hope that the Congress of the White and the Black, which has been instituted, will have great influence on the inhabitants of America, so that everyone may confess and bear witness that the teachings of Bahá'u'lláh assemble the Black, the White, the Yellow, the Red and the Brown under the shade of the pavilion of the oneness of the world of humanity; and that if His teachings be not enforced, the antagonism between the Black and the White in America will give rise to great calamities. The salve for this wound and the remedy for this disease are none other than the breaths of holiness. If the hearts be attracted to the heavenly bounties, surely the White and Black will, in a short time, according to the teachings of Bahá'u'lláh, put away hatred and animosity and establish love and fellowship.
' Abdu'l-Baha, *from a recently translated Tablet*

43. The body politic may be likened to the human organism. As long as the various members and parts of that organism are coordinated and cooperating in harmony, we have as a result the expression of life in its fullest degree. When these members lack coordination and harmony, we have the reverse, which in the human organism is disease, dissolution, death. Similarly, in the body politic of humanity dissension, discord and warfare are always destructive and inevitably fatal. All created beings are dependent upon peace and co-ordination, for every contingent and phenomenal being is a composition of distinct elements. As long as there is affinity and cohesion among these constituent elements, strength and life are manifest; but when dissension and repulsion arise among them, disintegration follows. This is proof that peace and amity, which God has willed for His children, are the sav--ing factors of human society, whereas war and strife, which violate His ordinances, are the cause of death and destruction.
  'Abdu'l-Bahá, *The Promulgation of Universal Peace*, pp. 98–99

44. Never indeed have their been such widespread and basic upheavals, whether in the social, economic or political spheres of human activity as those now going on in different parts of the world. Never have there been so many and varied sources of danger as those that now threaten the structure of society. The following words of Bahá'u'lláh are indeed significant as we pause to reflect upon the present state of a strangely disordered world: "How long will humanity persist in its waywardness? How long will injustice continue? How long is chaos and confusion to reign amongst men? How long will discord agitate the face of society? The winds of despair are, alas, blowing from every direction, and the strife that divides and afflicts the human race is daily increasing. The signs of impending convulsions and chaos can now be discerned, inasmuch as the prevailing order appears to be lamentably defective."
  Shoghi Effendi, *The World Order of Bahá'u'lláh*, p. 32

45. We belong to an organic unit and when one part of the organism suffers all the rest of the body will feel its consequence. This is in fact the reason why Bahá'u'lláh calls our attention to the unity of mankind.
        Shoghi Effendi, *Lights of Guidance*, p. 92

46. Races, alienated more than ever before, are filled with mistrust, humiliation and fear, and seem to prepare themselves for a fresh and fateful encounter.
        Shoghi Effendi, *Bahá'í Administration*, pp. 67–68

47. He hopes that especially in the Amity work you will be guided to do the very best, for that is the outstanding social problem of that country. If that issue remains and drags and the existing distrust among the colored and white be left to wax stronger, as the Master said, the streets will actually run with blood. From our point of view, this problem can only be tackled from a spiritual angle, for only by a spiritual awakening can this misunderstanding and prejudice vanish. We are often apt to follow the modern attitude of mind and consider economic issues the common denominator of all our problems. With their spiritual approach, the Bahá'ís could achieve more than any other movement.
        On behalf of Shoghi Effendi, *The Power of Unity*, p. 43

48. "This question of the union of the white and the black is very important," He ['Abdu'l-Bahá] warns, "for if it is not realized, erelong great difficulties will arise, and harmful results will follow." "If this matter remaineth without change," is yet another warning, "enmity will be increased day by day, and the final result will be hardship and may end in bloodshed."

    . . . Let them [the black and white races], while each is attempting to contribute its share to the solution of this perplexing problem, call to mind the warnings of 'Abdu'l-Bahá, and visualize, while there is yet time, the dire

consequences that must follow if this challenging and unhappy situation that faces the entire American nation is not definitely remedied.
>Shoghi Effendi, *The Advent of Divine Justice*, p. 33

49. Moreover, the country of which it forms a part is passing through a crisis which, in its spiritual, moral, social and political aspects, is of extreme seriousness—a seriousness which to a superficial observer is liable to be dangerously underestimated.

The steady and alarming deterioration in the standard of morality as exemplified by the appalling increase of crime, by political corruption in ever widening and ever higher circles, by the loosening of the sacred ties of marriage, by the inordinate craving for pleasure and diversion, and by the marked and progressive slackening of parental control, is no doubt the most arresting and distressing aspect of the decline that has set in, and can be clearly perceived, in the fortunes of the entire nation.

Parallel with this, and pervading all departments of life—an evil which the nation, and indeed all those within the capitalist system, though to a lesser degree, share with that state and its satellites regarded as the sworn enemies of that system—is the crass materialism, which lays excessive and ever-increasing emphasis on material well-being, forgetful of those things of the spirit on which alone a sure and stable foundation can be laid for human society. It is this same cancerous materialism, born originally in Europe, carried to excess in the North American continent, contaminating the Asiatic peoples and nations, spreading its ominous tentacles to the borders of Africa, and now invading its very heart, which Bahá'u'lláh in unequivocal and emphatic language denounced in His Writings, comparing it to a devouring flame and regarding it as the chief factor in precipitating the dire ordeals and world-shaking crises that must necessarily involve the burning of cities and the spread of terror and consternation in the hearts of men. Indeed a foretaste of the devastation which this consuming fire will wreak upon the world, and with which it will lay waste the cities of the nations participating in this tragic world-engulfing contest, has been afforded by the last World War, marking the second stage in the global havoc which humanity, forgetful of its God and heedless of the clear warnings uttered by His appointed Messenger for this day, must, alas, inevitably experience. It is this same all-pervasive, pernicious materialism against which the voice of the Center of Bahá'u'lláh's Covenant was raised, with pathetic persistence, from platform and pulpit, in His addresses to the heedless multitudes, which, on the morrow of His fateful visit to both Europe and America, found themselves suddenly swept into the vortex of a tempest which in its range and severity was unsurpassed in the world's history.

Collateral with this ominous laxity in morals, and this progressive stress laid on man's material pursuits and well-being, is the darkening of the political horizon, as witnessed by the widening of the gulf separating the protagonists of two antagonistic schools of thought which, however divergent in their ideologies, are to be commonly condemned by the upholders of the standard of the Faith of Bahá'u'lláh for their materialistic philosophies and their neglect of those spiritual values and eternal verities on which alone a stable and flourishing civilization can be ultimately established. The multiplication, the diversity and the increasing destructive power of armaments to which both sides, in this world contest, caught in a whirlpool of fear, suspicion and hatred, are rapidly contributing; the outbreak of two successive bloody conflicts, entangling still further the American nation in the affairs of a distracted world, entailing a considerable loss in blood and treasure, swelling the national budget and progressively depreciating the currency of the state; the confusion, the vacillation, the suspicions besetting the European and Asiatic nations in their attitude to the American nation; the overwhelming accretion of strength to the arch enemy of the system championed by the American Union in consequence of the realignment of the powers in the Asiatic continent and particularly in the Far East—these have, moreover, contributed their share, in recent years, to the deterioration of a situation which, if not remedied, is bound to involve the American nation in a catastrophe of undreamed-of dimensions and of untold consequences to the social structure, the standard and conception of the American people and government.

No less serious is the stress and strain imposed on the fabric of American society through the fundamental and persistent neglect, by the governed and governors alike, of the supreme, the inescapable and urgent duty—so repeatedly and graphically represented and stressed by 'Abdu'l-Bahá in His arraignment of the basic weaknesses in the social fabric of the nation—of remedying, while there is yet time, through a revolutionary change in the concept and attitude of the average white American toward his Negro fellow citizen, a situation which, if allowed to drift, will, in the words of 'Abdu'l-Bahá, cause the streets of American cities to run with blood, aggravating thereby the havoc which the fearful weapons of destruction, raining from the air, and amassed by a ruthless, a vigilant, a powerful and inveterate enemy, will wreak upon those same cities.

The American nation, of which the community of the Most Great Name forms as yet a negligible and infinitesimal part, stands, indeed, from whichever angle one observes its immediate fortunes, in grave peril. The woes and tribulations which threaten it are partly avoidable but mostly inevitable and God-sent, for by reason of them a government and people clinging tenaciously to the obsolescent doctrine of absolute sovereignty and upholding a political system, manifestly at variance with the needs of a world already contracted into a neighborhood and crying out for unity, will find itself purged of its anachronistic conceptions, and prepared to play a preponderating role, as foretold by 'Abdu'l-Bahá, in the hoisting of the standard of the Lesser Peace, in the unification of mankind, and in the establishment of a world federal government on this planet. These same fiery tribulations will not only firmly weld the American nation to its sister nations in both hemispheres, but will through their cleansing effect, purge it thoroughly of the accumulated dross which ingrained racial prejudice, rampant materialism, widespread ungodliness and moral laxity have combined, in the course of successive generations, to produce, and which have prevented her thus far from assuming the role of world spiritual leadership forecast by 'Abdu'l-Bahá's unerring pen—a role which she is bound to fulfill through travail and sorrow.

Shoghi Effendi, *The Citadel of Faith*, pp. 124–27

50. With reference to your question concerning the racial problem in America; although the American race problem is no less serious than the race question in Europe, particularly as regards the Jews, yet the Guardian is inclined to think that for the present there is little likelihood of its becoming as widespread and tragic as in such European countries as Germany, Poland and other Central European and Balkanic states. He feels convinced, however, that unless the racial question in America is vigorously and fearlessly tackled, grave disturbances, of both a social and political nature, will inevitably result.

On behalf of Shoghi Effendi, to an individual believer, 4/27/39

51. The recent riots in Los Angeles and other cities are one more compelling reminder of the warnings uttered repeatedly by 'Abdu'l-Bahá during His visit to North America, and frequently echoed by Shoghi Effendi in his writings, about

the dangerous consequences of racial prejudice. They also underscore the timeliness of the statement on racial unity which you issued at the Bahá'í National Convention in 1991.

In the wake of the disturbances which threaten to engulf other areas, we reiterate more strongly than before the encouragement we expressed for your campaign to combat racism in the United States. It is highly fitting that during this Holy Year, which marks the centenary of the ascension of the Manifestation of God Who made the oneness of humankind the pivotal principle and goal of His Faith, you should sally forth in a mighty effort to rally the forces which will in His Name and in obedience to His command assist in eradicating this evil from the fair name of your country.

Rest assured of our prayers at the Holy Shrines that your exertions may be divinely confirmed.

> The Universal House of Justice, to the National Assembly of the United States, 5/11/92

52. 'Abdu'l-Bahá said: ". . . If the races do not come to an agreement, there can be no question or doubt of bloodshed. When I was in America, I told the white and colored people that it was incumbent upon them to be united or else there would be the shedding of blood. I did not say more than this that they might not be saddened. But, indeed, there is a greater danger than only the shedding of blood. It is the destruction of America. Because aside from the racial prejudice there is another agitating factor. It is that of America's enemies. These enemies are agitating both sides, that is, they are stirring up the white race against the colored race and the colored race against the white race. But of this the Americans are submerged in the sea of ignorance. They will regret it. But of what use will their regret be after the destruction of America? Will it be of any use then?"

I told him of a letter which I had received from Chicago during the week, stating that two houses belonging to colored Bahá'ís had been bombed with dynamite. 'Abdu'l-Bahá said: "I foretell things before they happen and I write about them before they occur. The destruction of two or three houses is of no importance, but the importance lies in what is coming, which is the destruction of America. The Arabs have many proverbs. For instance, 'Heavy rains begin with drops before it pours,' and 'The dancer starts with shaking the shoulder, then the whole body.' Now is the time for the Americans to take up this matter and unite both the white and the colored races. Otherwise, hasten ye towards destruction! Hasten ye toward devastation!"

        Letter written by Zia M. Baghdádí, containing the reported words of 'Abdu'l-Bahá, *Star of the West*, vol. 12, no. 6, pp. 120–21

Four

Unity in Diversity

I. The Purpose and Value of Diversity

> *This diversity, this difference*
> *is like the naturally created dissimilarity and variety*
> *of the limbs and organs of the human body,*
> *for each one contributeth to the*
> *beauty, efficiency and perfection of the whole.*
> 'Abdu'l-Bahá

1. My hope is that the white and the black will be united in perfect love and fellowship, with complete unity and brotherhood. Associate with each other, think of each other, and be like a rose garden. Anyone who goes into a rose garden will see various roses, white, pink, yellow, red, all growing together and replete with adornment. Each one accentuates the beauty of the other. Were all of one color, the garden would be monotonous to the eye. If they were all white or yellow or red, the garden would lack variety and attractiveness; but when the colors are varied, white, pink, yellow, red, there will be the greatest beauty. Therefore, I hope that you will be like a rose garden. Although different in colors, yet—praise be to God!—you receive rays from the same sun. From one cloud the rain is poured upon you. You are under the training of one Gardener, and this Gardener is kind to all. Therefore, you must manifest the utmost kindness towards each other, and you may rest assured that whenever you are united, the confirmations of the Kingdom of Abhá will reach you, the

heavenly favors will descend, the bounties of God will be bestowed, the Sun of Reality will shine, the cloud of mercy will pour its showers, and the breeze of divine generosity will waft its fragrances upon you.

I hope you will continue in unity and fellowship. How beautiful to see blacks and whites together! I hope, God willing, the day may come when I shall see the red men, the Indians, with you, also Japanese and others. Then there will be white roses, yellow roses, red roses, and a very wonderful rose garden will appear in the world.
    'Abdu'l-Bahá, *The Promulgation of Universal Peace*, pp. 427–28

2. Be like a well-cultivated garden wherein the roses and variegated flowers of heaven are growing in fragrance and beauty. It is my hope that your hearts may become as ready ground, carefully tilled and prepared, upon which the divine showers of the bounties of the Blessed Perfection may descend and the zephyrs of this divine springtime may blow with quickening breath. Then will the garden of your hearts bring forth its flowers of delightful fragrance to refresh the nostril of the heavenly Gardener. Let your hearts reflect the glories of the Sun of Truth in their many colors to gladden the eye of the divine Cultivator Who has nourished them. Day by day become more closely attracted in order that the love of God may illumine all those with whom you come in contact. Be as one spirit, one soul, leaves of one tree, flowers of one garden, waves of one ocean.

As difference in degree of capacity exists upon human souls, as difference of capability is found, therefore, individualities will differ one from another. But in reality this is a reason for unity and not for discord and enmity. If the flowers of a garden were all of one color, the effect would be monotonous to the eye; but if the colors are variegated, it is most pleasing and wonderful. The difference in adornment of color and capacity of reflection among the flowers gives the garden its beauty and charm. Therefore, although we are of different individualities, different in ideas and of various fragrances, let us strive like flowers of the same divine garden to live together in harmony. Even though each soul has its own individual perfume and color, all are reflecting the same light, all contributing fragrance to the same breeze which blows through the garden, all continuing to grow in complete harmony and accord.

'Abdu'l-Bahá, *The Promulgation of Universal Peace*, p. 24

3. A meeting such as this seems like a beautiful cluster of precious jewels—pearls, rubies, diamonds, sapphires. It is a source of joy and delight. Whatever is conducive to the unity of the world of mankind is most acceptable and praiseworthy; whatever is the cause of discord and disunion is saddening and deplorable. Consider the significance of unity and harmony.

This evening I will speak to you upon the subject of existence and nonexistence, life and death. Existence is the expression and outcome of composition and combination. Nonexistence is the expression and outcome of division and disintegration. If we study the forms of existence in the material universe, we find that all created things are the result of composition. Material elements have grouped together in infinite variety and endless forms. Each organism is a compound; each object is an expression of elemental affinity. We find the complex human organism simply an aggregation of cellular structure; the tree is a composite of plant cells; the animal, a combination and grouping of cellular atoms or units, and so on. Existence or the expression of being is, therefore, composition; and nonexistence is decomposition, division, disintegration. When elements have been brought together in a certain plan of combination, the result is the human organism; when these elements separate and disperse, the outcome is death and nonexistence. Life is, therefore, the product of composition; and death signifies decomposition.

Likewise, in the world of minds and souls, fellowship, which is an expression of composition, is conducive to life, whereas discord, which is an expression of decomposition, is the equivalent of death. Without cohesion among the individual elements which compose the body politic, disintegration and decay must inevitably follow and life be extinguished.... Therefore, in the world of humanity it is wise and seemly that all the individual members should manifest unity and affinity. In the clustered jewels of the races may the blacks be as sapphires and rubies and the whites as diamonds and pearls. The composite beauty of humanity will be witnessed in their unity and blending. How glorious the spectacle of real unity among mankind! How conducive to peace, confidence and happiness if races and nations were united in fellowship and accord! The Prophets of God were sent into the world upon this mission of unity and agreement: that these long-separated sheep might flock together.
    'Abdu'l-Bahá, *The Promulgation of Universal Peace*, pp. 56–57

4. Praise be to God, today the splendor of the Word of God hath illumined every horizon, and from all sects, races, tribes, nations, and communities souls have come together in the light of the Word, assembled, united and agreed in perfect harmony. Oh! What a great number of meetings are held adorned with souls from various races and diverse sects! Anyone attending these will be struck with amazement, and might suppose that these souls are all of one land, one nationality, one community, one thought, one belief and one opinion; whereas, in fact, one is an American, the other an African, one cometh from Asia and another from Europe, one is a native of India, another is from Turkestan, one is an Arab, another a Tajik, another a Persian and yet another a Greek. Notwithstanding such diversity they associate in perfect

harmony and unity, love and freedom; they have one voice, one thought and one purpose.
 'Abdu'l-Bahá, *Selections from the Writings of 'Abdu'l-Bahá*, p. 292

5. It therefore becometh manifest that amity and cohesion are indicative of the training of the Real Educator, and dispersion and separation a proof of savagery and deprivation of divine education.

A critic may object, saying that peoples, races, tribes and communities of the world are of different and varied customs, habits, tastes, character, inclinations and ideas, that opinions and thoughts are contrary to one another, and how, therefore, is it possible for real unity to be revealed and perfect accord among human souls to exist?

In answer we say that differences are of two kinds. One is the cause of annihilation and is like the antipathy existing among warring nations and conflicting tribes who seek each other's destruction, uprooting one another's families, depriving one another of rest and comfort and unleashing carnage. The other kind which is a token of diversity is the essence of perfection and the cause of the appearance of the bestowals of the Most Glorious Lord.

Consider the flowers of a garden: though differing in kind, color, form and shape, yet, inasmuch as they are refreshed by the waters of one spring, revived by the breath of one wind, invigorated by the rays of one sun, this diversity increaseth their charm, and addeth unto their beauty. Thus when that unifying force, the penetrating influence of the Word of God, taketh effect, the difference of customs, manners, habits, ideas, opinions and dispositions embellisheth the world of humanity. This diversity, this difference is like the naturally created dissimilarity and variety of the limbs and organs of the human body, for each one contributeth to the beauty, efficiency and perfection of the whole. When these different limbs and organs come under the influence of man's sovereign soul, and the soul's power pervadeth the limbs and members, veins and arteries of the body, then difference reinforceth harmony, diversity strengtheneth love, and multiplicity is the greatest factor for coordination.

How unpleasing to the eye if all the flowers and plants, the leaves and blossoms, the fruits, the branches and the trees of that garden where all of the same shape and color! Diversity of hues, form and shape, enricheth and adorneth the garden, and heighteneth the effect thereof. In like manner, when divers shades of thought, temperament and character, are brought together under the power and influence of one central agency, the beauty and glory of human perfection will be revealed and made manifest.
'Abdu'l-Bahá, *Selections from the Writings of 'Abdu'l-Bahá*, pp. 290–92

6. Praise be to God, the hearts of the friends are united and linked together, whether they be from the east or the west, from north or from south, whether they be German, French, Japanese, American, and whether they pertain to the white, the black, the red, the yellow or the brown race. Variations of color, of land and of race are of no importance in the Bahá'í Faith; on the contrary, Bahá'í unity overcometh them all and doth away with all these fancies and imaginations.
'Abdu'l-Bahá, *Selections from the Writings of 'Abdu'l-Bahá*, p. 113

7. In marriage the more distant the blood-relationship the better, for such distance in family ties between husband and wife provides the basis for the well-being of humanity and is conducive to fellowship among mankind.
'Abdu'l-Bahá, *Power of Unity*, p. 55

8. God's wisdom hath decreed that partners to a marriage should be of distant origins. That is, the further removed the relationship between husband and wife is, the stronger, the more beautiful and the healthier will their offspring be.
'Abdu'l-Bahá, from a previously unpublished Tablet

II. The Principle of Unity in Diversity

> *The diversity in the human family*
> *should be the cause of love and harmony, as it is in music*
> *where many different notes blend together*
> *in the making of a perfect chord.*
> 'Abdu'l-Bahá

9. The Creator of all is One God.

From this same God all creation sprang into existence, and He is the one goal, towards which everything in nature yearns. This conception was embodied in the words of Christ, when He said, "I am the Alpha and the Omega, the beginning and the end." Man is the sum of Creation, and the Perfect Man is the expression of the complete thought of the Creator—the Word of God.

Consider the world of created beings, how varied and diverse they are in species, yet with one sole origin. All the differences that appear are those of outward form and color. This diversity of type is apparent throughout the whole of nature.

Behold a beautiful garden full of flowers, shrubs, and trees. Each flower has a different charm, a peculiar beauty, its own delicious perfume and beautiful color. The trees too, how varied are they in size, in growth, in foliage—and what different fruits they bear! Yet all these flowers, shrubs and trees spring from the self-same earth, the same sun shines upon them and the same clouds give them rain.

So it is with humanity. It is made up of many races, and its peoples are of different color, white, black, yellow, brown and red—but they all come from the same God, and all are servants to Him. This diversity among the children of men has unhappily not the same effect as it has among the vegetable creation, where the spirit shown is more harmonious. Among men exists the diversity of animosity, and it is this that causes war and hatred among the different nations of the world.

Differences which are only those of blood also cause them to destroy and kill one another. Alas! that this should still be so. Let us look rather at the beauty in diversity, the beauty of harmony, and learn a lesson from the vegetable creation. If you beheld a garden in which all the plants were the same as to form, color and perfume, it would not seem beautiful to you at all, but, rather, monotonous and dull. The garden which is pleasing to the eye and which makes the heart glad, is the garden in which are growing side by side flowers of every hue, form and perfume, and the joyous contrast of color is what makes for charm and beauty. So is it with trees. An orchard full of fruit trees is a delight; so is a plantation planted with many species of shrubs. It is just the diversity and variety that constitutes its charm; each flower, each tree, each fruit, besides being beautiful in itself, brings out by contrast the qualities of the others, and shows to advantage the special loveliness of each and all.

Thus should it be among the children of men! The diversity in the human family should be the cause of love and harmony, as it is in music where many different notes blend together in the making of a perfect chord. If you meet those of different race and color from yourself, do not mistrust them and withdraw yourself into your shell of conventionality, but rather be glad and show them kindness. Think of them as different colored roses growing in the beautiful garden of humanity, and rejoice to be among them.

Likewise, when you meet those whose opinions differ from your own, do not turn away your face from them. All are seeking truth, and there are many roads leading thereto. Truth has many aspects, but it remains always and forever one.

Do not allow difference of opinion, or diversity of thought to separate you from your fellowmen, or to be the cause of dispute, hatred and strife in your hearts.

Rather, search diligently for the truth and make all men your friends.
 'Abdu'l-Bahá, *Paris Talks*, pp. 51–53

10. It is clear that the reality of mankind is diverse, that opinions are various and sentiments different; and this difference of opinions, of thoughts, of intelligence, of sentiments among the human species, arises from essential necessity; for the differences in the degrees of existence of creatures is one of the necessities of existence, which unfolds itself in infinite forms. Therefore we have need of a general power which may dominate the sentiments, the opinions, and the thoughts of all, thanks to which these divisions may no longer have effect, and all individuals may be brought under the influence of the unity of the world of humanity.
 'Abdu'l-Bahá, *Some Answered Questions*, pp. 345–46

11. Bahá'u'lláh has proclaimed the oneness of the world of humanity. He has caused various nations and divergent creeds to unite. He has declared that difference of race and color is like the variegated beauty of flowers in a garden. If you enter a garden, you will see yellow, white, blue, red flowers in profusion and beauty—each radiant within itself and although different from the others, lending its own charm to them. Racial difference in the human kingdom is similar. If all the flowers in a garden were of the same color, the effect would be monotonous and wearying to the eye.

 Therefore, Bahá'u'lláh hath said that the various races of humankind lend a composite harmony and beauty of color to the whole. Let all associate, therefore, in this great human garden even as flowers grow and blend together side by side without discord or disagreement between them.
 'Abdu'l-Bahá, *The Promulgation of Universal Peace*, pp. 68–69

12. Thou hast written that there were several joyful and happy meetings—some for the white and some for the black.

However, both races, praise be to God, are under the protection of the All-Knowing God; therefore, the lamps of unity must be lighted in these meetings in such a manner that no distinction may be perceived between the white and the black. Colors are nonessential characteristics, but the realities of men are essential. When there is unity of the essence, what power hath the ephemeral? When the light of reality is shining, what power hath the darkness of the unreal? If it be possible, gather together these two races—black and white—into one Assembly, and create such a love in the hearts that they shall not only unite, but blend into one reality. Know thou of a certainty that as a result differences and disputes between black and white will be totally abolished. By the Will of God, may it be so! This is a most great service to humanity.
 'Abdu'l-Bahá, *The Power of Unity*, pp. 67–68

13. When a person becomes a Bahá'í, he gives up the past only in the sense that he is a part of this new and living Faith of God, and must seek to pattern himself, in act and thought, along the lines laid down by Bahá'u'lláh. The fact that he is by origin a Jew or a Christian, a black man or a white man, is not important any more, but, as you say, lends color and charm to the Bahá'í community in that it demonstrates unity in diversity.
 On behalf of Shoghi Effendi, to an individual believer, 3/12/49, *Bahá'í News*, no. 251, p. 2

14. . . . the Cause is for every nation, not just America, and each people can and must contribute some of the finest elements of its own genius and race to the Faith.
 On behalf of Shoghi Effendi, to an individual believer, 8/19/52

15. You ask about the criteria for establishment of National Spiritual Assemblies. The decisions about the formation in any country or region of a National Spiritual Assembly, and

the area of jurisdiction of the National Assembly, are assigned to the Universal House of Justice in Section IV of the By-laws forming part of the Constitution of the Universal House of Justice. However, it should be noted that the existence of a group of believers sharing a distinct culture is not sufficient reason to form a National Spiritual Assembly. Rather, the Bahá'í Faith aims to demonstrate its power to create unified organic units in which cultural diversity is fostered, which are free from parochial attitudes and from ethnic or cultural prejudices, and in which all believers regard each other as true brothers and sisters. As the Faith progresses, the contrast is growing in many parts of the world, between the fragmented and mutually-antagonistic elements of society on the one hand, and the unified and harmonious Bahá'í community on the other hand.

    The Universal House of Justice, to Bahá'ís in the United States, 7/25/88

III. Maintaining Diversity

The Bahá'í Faith
seeks to maintain cultural diversity
while promoting the unity of all peoples.
Indeed, such diversity will enrich the tapestry of human life
in a peaceful world society.
The Universal House of Justice

16. Let there be no misgivings as to the animating purpose of the worldwide Law of Bahá'u'lláh. Far from aiming at the subversion of the existing foundations of society, it seeks to broaden its basis, to remold its institutions in a manner consonant with the needs of an ever-changing world. It can conflict with no legitimate allegiances, nor can it undermine essential loyalties. Its purpose is neither to stifle the flame of a sane and intelligent patriotism in men's hearts, nor to

abolish the system of national autonomy so essential if the evils of excessive centralization are to be avoided. It does not ignore, nor does it attempt to suppress, the diversity of ethnical origins, of climate, of history, of language and tradition, of thought and habit, that differentiate the peoples and nations of the world. It calls for a wider loyalty, for a larger aspiration than any that has animated the human race. It insists upon the subordination of national impulses and interests to the imperative claims of a unified world. It repudiates excessive centralization on one hand, and disclaims all attempts at uniformity on the other. Its watchword is unity in diversity. . . .
    Shoghi Effendi, *The World Order of Bahá'u'lláh*, pp. 41–42

17. The unity of the human race, as envisaged by Bahá'u'lláh, implies the establishment of a world commonwealth in which all nations, races, creeds and classes are closely and permanently united, and in which the autonomy of its state members and the personal freedom and initiative of the individuals that compose them are definitely and completely safeguarded.
    Shoghi Effendi, *The World Order of Bahá'u'lláh*, p. 203

18. The Guardian was very pleased to learn of the progress done by the Indian National Spiritual Assembly in its efforts to consolidate, widen and maintain the scope of its national activities. The difficulties in your way are tremendous. The differences of language and of social and intellectual background do, undoubtedly, render the work somewhat difficult to carry out and may temporarily check the efficient and smooth working of the national administrative machinery of the Faith. They, nevertheless, impart to the deliberations of the National Assembly a universality which they would be otherwise lacking, and give to its members a breadth of view which is their duty to cultivate and foster. It is not uniformity which we should seek in the formation of any national or

local assembly. For the bedrock of the Bahá'í administrative order is the principle of unity in diversity, which has been so strongly and so repeatedly emphasized in the writings of the Cause. Differences which are not fundamental and contrary to the basic teachings of the Cause should be maintained, while the underlying unity of the administrative order should be at any cost preserved and insured.
    On behalf of Shoghi Effendi, *Dawn of a New Day*, pp. 47–48

19. We stand for unity through diversity and we hold in contempt every attempt at uniformity or at complete separateness.
    On behalf of Shoghi Effendi, to an individual believer, 6/3/33

20. Bahá'ís should obviously be encouraged to preserve their inherited cultural identities, as long as the activities involved do not contravene the principles of the Faith. The perpetuation of such cultural characteristics is an expression of unity in diversity.
    On behalf of The Universal House of Justice, *Developing Distinctive Bahá'í Communities*, 9.25

21. The Bahá'í Faith seeks to maintain cultural diversity while promoting the unity of all peoples. Indeed, such diversity will enrich the tapestry of human life in a peaceful world society. The House of Justice supports the view that in every country it is quite appropriate for the cultural traditions of the people to be observed within the Bahá'í community as long as they are not contrary to the teachings. The general attitude of the Faith towards the traditional practices of various peoples is expressed in the following statement of Shoghi Effendi's, published in *The World Order of Bahá'u'lláh*, U.S. 1982 edition, pages 41–42.

    "Let there be no misgivings as to the animating purpose of the worldwide Law of Bahá'u'lláh.... It does not ignore, nor does it attempt to suppress, the diversity of ethnical origins, of climate, of history, of language and tradition, of thought and habit, that differentiate the peoples and nations of the world. . . . Its watchword is unity in diversity such as 'Abdu'l-Bahá Himself has explained:

"'Consider the flowers of a garden. . . . Diversity of hues, form and shape enricheth and adorneth the garden, and heighteneth the effect thereof.'"

Of course, many cultural elements everywhere inevitably will disappear or be merged with related ones from their societies, yet the totality will achieve that promised diversity within world unity. We can expect much cultural diversity in the long period before the emergence of a world commonwealth of nations in the Golden Age of Peace of Bahá'u'lláh's new world order. Much wisdom and tolerance will be required, and much time must elapse until the advent of that great day.

At the present time, the challenge to every Bahá'í community is to avoid suppression of those culturally-diverse elements which are not contrary to the teachings, while establishing and maintaining such a high degree of unity that others are attracted to the Cause of God.

> The Universal House of Justice, to individual believers in the United States, 7/25/88

Five

Applying Solutions to Racism

I. The Most Vital and Challenging Issue: Goal and Responsibilities

> *Verily, God has chosen you for His love and knowledge;*
> *God has chosen you for the worthy service of unifying mankind;*
> *God has chosen you for the purpose of investigating reality*
> *and promulgating international peace;*
> *God has chosen you for the progress and development of humanity,*
> *for spreading and proclaiming true education,*
> *for the expression of love toward your fellow creatures*
> *and the removal of prejudice;*
> *God has chosen you to blend together human hearts*
> *and give light to the human world.*
> 'Abdu'l-Bahá

1. O contending peoples and kindreds of the earth! Set your faces towards unity, and let the radiance of its light shine upon you. Gather ye together, and for the sake of God resolve to root out whatever is the source of contention amongst you.
Bahá'u'lláh, *Gleanings*, p. 217

2. Strive with heart and soul in order to bring about union and harmony among the white and the black and prove thereby the unity of the Bahá'í world wherein distinction of color findeth no place, but where hearts only are considered.
'Abdu'l-Bahá, *Selections from the Writings of 'Abdu'l-Bahá*, pp. 112–13

3. In all matters, endeavor not to cause grief to any one. Strive firmly to establish unity and harmony. The least difference today may cause great difference in the future.

O ye beloved ones of God! The manifestation of the Light of Unity is for binding together the people of the world. If this unity is not attained, the tree of life is made fruitless, the heavenly bounty is not utilized. The blessed blood (of the saints) was shed for bringing about unity and harmony. These souls gave their lives as sacrifice in order to produce the love that bindeth the hearts of all the people. Therefore, ye should all spend your efforts in uniting and reconciling (the people), so that the light of God's love may permeate the universe.
'Abdu'l-Bahá, *Tablets of 'Abdu'l-Bahá*, p. 21

4. Until such time, however, as the friends establish perfect unity among themselves, how can they summon others to harmony and peace?
'Abdu'l-Bahá, *Selections from the Writings of 'Abdu'l-Bahá*, p. 277

5. If this Cause cannot unite two individuals, how can we expect it to unite the world?
Shoghi Effendi, quoted in *Bahá'í News*, #13, 9/26, p.3

6. Many holy souls in former times longed to witness this century, lamenting night and day, yearning to be upon the earth in this cycle; but our presence and privilege is the beneficent gift of the Lord. In His divine mercy and absolute virtue He has bestowed this upon us, even as Christ declared, "Many are called but few are chosen." Verily, God has chosen you for His love and knowledge; God has chosen you for the worthy service of unifying mankind; God has chosen you for the purpose of investigating reality and promulgating international peace; God has chosen you for the progress and development of humanity, for spreading and proclaiming

true education, for the expression of love toward your fellow creatures and the removal of prejudice; God has chosen you to blend together human hearts and give light to the human world.
    'Abdu'l-Bahá, *The Promulgation of Universal Peace*, pp. 334–35

7. Thou must endeavor that they intermarry. There is no greater means to bring about affection between the white and the black than the influence of the Word of God. Likewise marriage between these two races will wholly destroy and eradicate the root of enmity.
    'Abdu'l-Bahá, *The Power of Unity*, p. 55

8. O ye two who have believed in Him!
    ... I pray God that ye may at all times be in the utmost love and harmony, and be a cause for the spirituality of the human world. This union will unquestionably promote love and affection between the black and the white, and will affect and encourage others. These two races will unite and merge together, and there will appear and take root a new generation sound in health and beauteous in countenance.
    'Abdu'l-Bahá, *The Power of Unity*, p. 55

9. . . . . [freedom from prejudice of race, class, creed or color] should be the immediate, the universal, and the chief concern of all and sundry members of the Bahá'í community, of whatever age, rank, experience, class, or color, as all, with no exception, must face its challenging implications, and none can claim, however much he may have progressed along this line, to have completely discharged the stern responsibilities which it inculcates.
    Shoghi Effendi, *The Advent of Divine Justice*, pp. 18–19

10. The Most Challenging Issue[†]

As to racial prejudice, the corrosion of which, for well nigh a century, has bitten into the fiber, and attacked the whole social structure of American society, it should be regarded as constituting the most vital and challenging issue confronting the Bahá'í community at the present stage of its evolution. The ceaseless exertions which this issue of paramount importance calls for, the sacrifices it must impose, the care and vigilance it demands, the moral courage and fortitude it requires, the tact and sympathy it necessitates, invest this problem, which the American believers are still far from having satisfactorily resolved, with an urgency and importance that cannot be overestimated. White and Negro, high and low, young and old, whether newly converted to the Faith or not, all who stand identified with it must participate in, and lend their assistance, each according to his or her capacity, experience, and opportunities, to the common task of fulfilling the instructions, realizing the hopes, and following the example, of 'Abdu'l-Bahá. Whether colored or non-colored, neither race has the right, or can conscientiously claim, to be regarded as absolved from such an obligation, as having realized such hopes, or having faithfully followed such an example. A long and thorny road, beset with pitfalls, still remains untraveled, both by the white and the Negro exponents of the redeeming Faith of Bahá'u'lláh. On the distance they cover, and the manner in which they travel that road, must depend, to an extent which few among them can imagine, the operation of those intangible influences which are indispensable to the spiritual triumph of the

---

[†] The entire text of this section of *The Advent of Divince Justice* is reproduced here. To assist in clarifying the specific tasks assigned to Baha'is of African and European descent, certain portions of it are repeated in subsequent and other sections of this publication.

American believers and the material success of their newly launched enterprise.

Let them call to mind, fearlessly and determinedly, the example and conduct of 'Abdu'l-Bahá while in their midst. Let them remember His courage, His genuine love, His informal and indiscriminating fellowship, His contempt for and impatience of criticism, tempered by His tact and wisdom. Let them revive and perpetuate the memory of those unforgettable and historic episodes and occasions on which He so strikingly demonstrated His keen sense of justice, His spontaneous sympathy for the downtrodden, His ever-abiding sense of the oneness of the human race, His overflowing love for its members, and His displeasure with those who dared to flout His wishes, to deride His methods, to challenge His principles, or to nullify His acts.

To discriminate against any race, on the ground of its being socially backward, politically immature, and numerically in a minority, is a flagrant violation of the spirit that animates the Faith of Bahá'u'lláh. The consciousness of any division or cleavage in its ranks is alien to its very purpose, principles, and ideals. Once its members have fully recognized the claim of its Author, and, by identifying themselves with its Administrative Order, accepted unreservedly the principles and laws embodied in its teachings, every differentiation of class, creed, or color must automatically be obliterated, and never be allowed, under any pretext, and however great the pressure of events or of public opinion, to reassert itself. If any discrimination is at all to be tolerated, it should be a discrimination not against, but rather in favor of the minority, be it racial or otherwise. Unlike the nations and peoples of the earth, be they of the East or of the West, democratic or authoritarian, communist or capitalist, whether belonging to the Old World or the New, who either ignore, trample upon, or extirpate, the racial, religious, or political minorities within the sphere of their jurisdiction, every organized community enlisted under the banner of Bahá'u'lláh should feel it to be its first and inescapable obligation to nurture, encourage, and safeguard every minority belonging to any faith, race, class, or nation within it. So great and vital is this principle that in such circumstances, as when an equal number of ballots have been cast in an election, or where the qualifications for any office are balanced as between the various races, faiths or nationalities within the community, priority should unhesitatingly be accorded the party representing the minority, and this for no other reason except to stimulate and encourage it, and afford it an opportunity to further the interests of the community. In the light of this principle, and bearing in mind the extreme desirability of having the minority elements participate and share responsibility in the conduct of Bahá'í activity, it should be the duty of every Bahá'í community so to arrange its affairs that in cases where individuals belonging to the divers minority elements within it are already qualified and fulfill the necessary requirements, Bahá'í representative institutions, be they Assemblies, conventions, conferences, or committees, may have represented on them as many of these divers elements, racial or otherwise, as possible. The adoption of such a course, and faithful adherence to it, would not only be a source of inspiration and encouragement to those elements that are numerically small and inadequately represented, but would demonstrate to the world at large the universality and representative character of the Faith of Bahá'u'lláh, and the freedom of His followers from the taint of those prejudices which have already wrought such havoc in the domestic affairs, as well as the foreign relationships, of the nations.

    Freedom from racial prejudice, in any of its forms, should, at such a time as this when an increasingly large section of the human race is falling a victim to its devastating ferocity, be adopted as the watchword of the entire body of the American believers, in whichever state they reside, in whatever circles they move, whatever their age, traditions, tastes, and habits. It should be consistently demonstrated in every phase of their activity and life, whether in the Bahá'í community or outside it, in public or in private, formally as well as informally, individually as well as in their official capacity as organized groups, committees and Assemblies. It should be deliberately cultivated through the various and everyday opportunities, no matter how insignificant, that present themselves, whether in their homes, their business offices, their schools and colleges, their social parties and recreation grounds, their Bahá'í meetings, conferences, conventions, summer schools and Assemblies. It should, above all else, become the keynote of the policy of that august body which, in its capacity as the national representative, and the director and coordinator of the affairs of the community, must set the example, and facilitate the application of such a vital principle to the lives and activities of those whose interests it safeguards and represents.

"O ye discerning ones!" Bahá'u'lláh has written, "Verily, the words which have descended from the heaven of the Will of God are the source of unity and harmony for the world. Close your eyes to racial differences, and welcome all with the light of oneness." "We desire but the good of the world and the happiness of the nations," He proclaims, "... that all nations should become one in faith and all men as brothers; that the bonds of affection and unity between the sons of men should be strengthened; that diversity of religion should cease, and differences of race be annulled." "Bahá'u'lláh hath said," writes 'Abdu'l-Bahá, "that the various races of humankind lend a composite harmony and beauty of color to the whole. Let all associate, therefore, in this great human garden even as flowers grow and blend together side by side without discord or disagreement between them." "Bahá'u'lláh," 'Abdu'l-Bahá moreover has said, "once compared the colored people to the black pupil of the eye surrounded by the white. In this black pupil is seen the reflection of that which is before it, and through it the light of the spirit shineth forth."

"God," 'Abdu'l-Bahá Himself declares, "maketh no distinction between the white and the black. If the hearts are pure both are acceptable unto Him. God is no respecter of persons on account of either color or race. All colors are acceptable unto Him, be they white, black, or yellow. Inasmuch as all were created in the image of God, we must bring ourselves to realize that all embody divine possibilities." "In the estimation of God," He states, "all men are equal. There is no distinction or preference for any soul, in the realm of His justice and equity." "God did not make these divisions," He affirms; "these divisions have had their origin in man himself. Therefore, as they are against the plan and purpose of God they are false and imaginary." "In the estimation of God," He again affirms, "there is no distinction of color; all are one in the color and beauty of servitude to Him. Color is not important; the heart is all-important. It mattereth not what the exterior may be if the heart is pure and white within. God doth not behold differences of hue and complexion. He looketh at the hearts. He whose morals and virtues are praiseworthy is preferred in the presence of God; he who is devoted to the Kingdom is most beloved. In the realm of genesis and creation the question of color is of least importance."

"Throughout the animal kingdom," He explains, "we do not find the creatures separated because of color. They recognize unity of species and oneness of kind. If we do not find color distinction drawn in a kingdom of lower intelligence and reason, how can it be justified among human beings, especially when we know that all have come from the same source and belong to the same household? In origin and intention of creation mankind is one. Distinctions of race and color have arisen afterward." "Man is endowed with superior reasoning power and the faculty of perception"; He further explains, "he is the manifestation of divine bestowals. Shall racial ideas prevail and obscure the creative purpose of unity in his kingdom?" "One of the important questions," He significantly remarks, "which affect the unity and the solidarity of mankind is the fellowship and equality of the white and colored races. Between these two races certain points of agreement and points of distinction exist which warrant just and mutual consideration. The points of contact are many.... In this country, the United States of America, patriotism is common to both races; all have equal rights to citizenship, speak one language, receive the blessings of the same civilization, and follow the precepts of the same religion. In fact numerous points of partnership and agreement exist between the two races, whereas the one point of distinction is that of color. Shall this, the least of all distinctions, be allowed to separate you as races and individuals?" "This variety in forms and coloring," He stresses, "which is manifest in all the kingdoms is according to creative Wisdom and hath a divine purpose." "The diversity in the human family," He claims, "should be the cause of love and harmony, as it is in music where many different notes blend together in the making of a perfect chord." "If you meet," is His admonition, "those of a different race and color from yourself, do not mistrust them, and withdraw yourself into your shell of conventionality, but rather be glad and show them kindness." "In the world of being," He testifies, "the meeting is blessed when the white and colored races meet together with infinite spiritual love and heavenly harmony. When such meetings are established, and the participants associate with each other with perfect love, unity and kindness, the angels of the Kingdom praise them, and the Beauty of Bahá'u'lláh addresseth them, 'Blessed are ye! Blessed are ye!'" "When a gathering of these two races is brought about," He likewise asserts, "that assemblage will become the magnet of the Concourse on high, and the confirmation of the Blessed

Beauty will surround it." "Strive earnestly," He again exhorts both races, "and put forth your greatest endeavor toward the accomplishment of this fellowship and the cementing of this bond of brotherhood between you. Such an attainment is not possible without will and effort on the part of each; from one, expressions of gratitude and appreciation; from the other, kindliness and recognition of equality. Each one should endeavor to develop and assist the other toward mutual advancement. . . . Love and unity will be fostered between you, thereby bringing about the oneness of mankind. For the accomplishment of unity between the colored and white will be an assurance of the world's peace." "I hope," He thus addresses members of the white race, "that ye may cause that downtrodden race to become glorious, and to be joined with the white race, to serve the world of man with the utmost sincerity, faithfulness, love, and purity. This opposition, enmity, and prejudice among the white race and the colored cannot be effaced except through faith, assurance, and the teachings of the Blessed Beauty." "This question of the union of the white and the black is very important," He warns, "for if it is not realized, erelong great difficulties will arise, and harmful results will follow." "If this matter remaineth without change," is yet another warning, "enmity will be increased day by day, and the final result will be hardship and may end in bloodshed."

A tremendous effort is required by both races if their outlook, their manners, and conduct are to reflect, in this darkened age, the spirit and teachings of the Faith of Bahá'u'lláh. Casting away once and for all the fallacious doctrine of racial superiority, with all its attendant evils, confusion, and miseries, and welcoming and encouraging the intermixture of races, and tearing down the barriers that now divide them, they should each endeavor, day and night, to fulfill their particular responsibilities in the common task which so urgently faces them. Let them, while each is attempting to contribute its share to the solution of this perplexing problem, call to mind the warnings of 'Abdu'l-Bahá, and visualize, while there is yet time, the dire consequences that must follow if this challenging and unhappy situation that faces the entire American nation is not definitely remedied.

Let the white make a supreme effort in their resolve to contribute their share to the solution of this problem, to abandon once for all their usually inherent and at times subconscious sense of superiority, to correct their tendency towards revealing a patronizing attitude towards the members of the other race, to persuade them through their intimate, spontaneous and informal association with them of the genuineness of their friendship and the sincerity of their intentions, and to master their impatience of any lack of responsiveness on the part of a people who have received, for so long a period, such grievous and slow-healing wounds. Let the Negroes, through a corresponding effort on their part, show by every means in their power the warmth of their response, their readiness to forget the past, and their ability to wipe out every trace of suspicion that may still linger in their hearts and minds. Let neither think that the solution of so vast a problem is a matter that exclusively concerns the other. Let neither think that such a problem can either easily or immediately be resolved. Let neither think that they can wait confidently for the solution of this problem until the initiative has been taken, and the favorable circumstances created, by agencies that stand outside the orbit of their Faith. Let neither think that anything short of genuine love, extreme patience, true humility, consummate tact, sound initiative, mature wisdom, and deliberate, persistent, and prayerful effort, can succeed in blotting out the stain which this patent evil has left on the fair name of their common country. Let them rather believe, and be firmly convinced, that on their mutual understanding, their amity, and sus-

tained cooperation, must depend, more than on any other force or organization operating outside the circle of their Faith, the deflection of that dangerous course so greatly feared by 'Abdu'l-Bahá, and the materialization of the hopes He cherished for their joint contribution to the fulfillment of that country's glorious destiny.
Shoghi Effendi, *The Advent of Divine Justice*, pp. 28–34

11. I have also received and read with the keenest interest and appreciation a copy of that splendid document formulated by the National Committee on interracial amity and addressed to all the Spiritual Assemblies throughout the United States and Canada. This moving appeal, so admirable in its conception, so sound and sober in its language, has struck a responsive chord in my heart. Sent forth at a highly opportune moment in the evolution of our sacred Faith, it has served as a potent reminder of these challenging issues which still confront in a peculiar manner the American believers.

As this problem, in the inevitable course of events, grows in acuteness and complexity, and as the number of the faithful from both races multiplies, it will become increasingly evident that the future growth and prestige of the Cause are bound to be influenced to a very considerable degree by the manner in which the adherents of the Bahá'í Faith carry out, first among themselves and in their relations with their fellowmen, those high standards of interracial amity so widely proclaimed and so fearlessly exemplified to the American people by our Master 'Abdu'l-Bahá.

I direct my appeal with all the earnestness and urgency that this pressing problem calls for to every conscientious upholder of the universal principles of Bahá'u'lláh to face this extremely delicate situation with the boldness, the decisiveness and wisdom it demands. I cannot believe that those whose hearts have been touched by the regenerating influence of God's creative Faith in His day will find it difficult to cleanse their souls from every lingering trace of racial animosity so subversive of the Faith they profess. How can hearts that throb with the love of God fail to respond to all the implications of this supreme injunction of Bahá'u'lláh, the unreserved acceptance of which, under the circumstances now prevailing in America, constitutes the hallmark of a true Bahá'í character?

Let every believer, desirous to witness the swift and healthy progress of the Cause of God, realize the twofold nature of his task. Let him first turn his eyes inwardly and search his own heart and satisfy himself that in his relations with his fellow-believers, irrespective of color and class, he is proving himself increasingly loyal to the spirit of his beloved Faith. Assured and content that he is exerting his utmost in a conscious effort to approach nearer every day the lofty station to which his gracious Master summons him, let him turn to his second task, and, with befitting confidence and vigor, assail the devastating power of those forces which in his own heart he has already succeeded in subduing. Fully alive to the unfailing efficacy of the power of Bahá'u'lláh, and armed with the essential weapons of wise restraint and inflexible resolve, let him wage a constant fight against the inherited tendencies, the corruptive instincts, the fluctuating fashions, the false pretences of the society in which he lives and moves.

In their relations amongst themselves as fellow-believers, let them not be content with the mere exchange of cold and empty formalities often connected with the organizing of banquets, receptions, consultative assemblies, and lecture-halls. Let them rather, as equal co-sharers in the spiritual benefits conferred upon them by Bahá'u'lláh, arise and, with the aid and counsel of their local and national representatives, supplement these official functions with those opportunities which only a close and intimate social intercourse can adequately provide. In their homes, in their hours of relaxation and leisure, in the daily contact of business transactions, in the association of their children, whether in their study-classes, their playgrounds, and club-rooms, in short under all possible circumstances, however insignificant they appear, the community of the followers of Bahá'u'lláh should satisfy themselves that in the eyes of the world at large and in the sight of their vigilant Master they are the living witnesses of those truths which He fondly cherished and tirelessly championed to the very end of His days. If we relax in our purpose, if we falter in our faith, if we neglect the varied opportunities given us from time to time by an all-wise and gracious Master, we are not merely failing in what is our most vital and conspicuous obligation, but are thereby insensibly retarding the flow of those quickening energies which can alone insure the vigorous and speedy development of God's struggling Faith.

I would particularly address my appeal to you, as the Trustees of God's sacred Faith, to reaffirm by word and deed the spirit and character of the insistent admonitions of 'Abdu'l-Bahá, so solemnly and so explicitly uttered in the course of His journeys through your land—a trust which it is your privilege and function to preserve and fortify.

> Shoghi Effendi, *Bahá'í Administration*, pp. 129–31

12. Both sides have prejudices to overcome; one, the prejudice which is built up in the minds of a people who have conquered and imposed their will, and the other the reactionary prejudice of those who have been conquered and sorely put upon.

> On behalf of Shoghi Effendi, in *To Move the World*, p. 294

13. He does not doubt—though it grieves him to have to admit it—that there are believers who have not overcome their racial prejudices. The Bahá'ís are not perfect, but they have made a great step forward by embracing the Faith of

God. We must be patient with each other, and realize that each one of us has some faults to overcome, of one kind or another.

You, he feels need to use greater wisdom and forbearance in dealing with your fellow-Bahá'ís and with difficult situations. To be courageous—as you evidently are—to rebel against the injustices of race prejudice and fight them, is not enough, you must also show some patience for those who suffer from this terrible American ailment of Negro prejudice and act with wisdom in overcoming it, instead of going at it so vehemently that you alienate the Bahá'ís, instead of leading them to greater manifestations of the Bahá'í spirit of brotherhood and racial amity. . . .
On behalf of Shoghi Effendi, *Lights of Guidance*, pp. 409–10

14. It is difficult for the friends to always remember that in matter[s] where race enters, a hundred times more consideration and wisdom in handling situations is necessary than when an issue is not complicated by this factor.
On behalf of Shoghi Effendi, to individual believers, 3/25/49

15. The Guardian feels that the Bahá'ís must take a very firm stand in maintaining the Bahá'í position with regard to the oneness of mankind. He feels that newspaper publicity is satisfactory, but the local assembly in each instance must approve it.

The oneness of mankind is the fundamental basis upon which the World Order of Bahá'u'lláh is built. Therefore the Bahá'ís must carry into their lives and into their activities the ideals which Bahá'u'lláh has taught of the unity of the human race.

At such a time as this the believers must take a very firm and strong stand on the racial issue so that there may be no misunderstanding on anyone's part as to just how the Bahá'ís view this all-important subject.

This does not mean that the Bahá'ís should enter into specific controversies which may rage; but it does mean that we should take our stand in behalf of the unity of the human family and the oneness of mankind; and there is no reason why we should not let the people know. This of course requires great consideration and consultation amongst the believers and particularly the local Assemblies in the areas involved.

The Guardian is praying that this serious problem may find solution in the hearts of the people because its ultimate solution rests with the individual who has become imbued with the ideal of unity and in that field there is no place for segregation.

> Shoghi Effendi, to an individual believer, *Bahá'í News*, no. 324, 2/58, p. 4

16. ... as you no doubt know, Bahá'u'lláh has stated that the purpose of marriage is to promote unity, so you should bear this in mind when dealing with your non-Bahá'í relatives; they cannot be expected to feel the way we do on questions of racial amity, and we must not force our views on them, but rather lovingly and wisely seek to educate them.

> On behalf of Shoghi Effendi, to an individual believer, 8/30/57

17. Another vital problem in America is the color question. Just as in Germany the racial problem is a real challenge to the German believers, so also in the States this problem for the colored and the white is a challenge to the American Bahá'ís. While the colored Bahá'ís must have more confidence in the white, the latter must, in their turn, and particularly on informal occasions, show more consideration and friendliness towards the former. The Bahá'í attitude towards this problem must in all cases be made definite and clear, although its solution requires a great measure of tact and wisdom.

> On behalf of Shoghi Effendi, to an individual believer, 3/16/34

18. Now, as to the methods which the friends should adopt for the application of this principle [of the oneness of mankind]; the Guardian has invariably urged the believers to act with the utmost wisdom, tact and moderation. It is not only fruitless, but actually harmful to the best interests of the Cause to publicly and violently attack the racial corruptions and traditions prevalent among such a large section of the American people. The friends should first start by applying the principle of the oneness of races within their own community, and thus set before the world outside a noble and inspiring example. Every trace of racial prejudice should be banished by the friends in their community life, and also in their private life, so much so that they should come to gradually forget the very existence of the racial problem as such. Such an attitude is bound to strongly impress every outsider and draw his attention to the Cause, and convince him of the sublimity and practicability of its Teachings.
    On behalf of Shoghi Effendi, to an individual believer, 11/11/36

19. He was . . . very happy to learn of the services you are rendering to the Cause in the way of bringing together the colored and white and creating between them the true spirit of love and brotherhood advocated by Bahá'u'lláh. . . . This amity work should be done especially among the young people for they have less prejudice to overcome and less conventions to draw them back and hamper their way.
    On behalf of Shoghi Effendi, to an individual believer, 4/6/32

20. He was especially glad to hear that the activities of the friends in eliminating racial differences is daily increasing and that they are achieving much more than in past days. Such progress is naturally very slow for there are strong feelings on both sides that have to be overcome. It is a training that must spread over a period of many years. Shoghi Effendi

hopes that the Bahá'ís will gradually be considered the leading religious movement working for this aim. This forms an important element in the teachings of Bahá'u'lláh and 'Abdu'l-Bahá and the world at large should know that it is so.
On behalf of Shoghi Effendi, to an individual believer, 3/11/31

21. All over the world the fires of prejudice are kindled, as if they would burn their brightest in defiance of the new order of oneness of mankind which Bahá'u'lláh has brought. The Bahá'ís face a tremendous task—but a task in which they know they will be victorious. They must demonstrate among themselves that they have done away with all sense of the false barriers which hitherto have kept men apart; then others will believe them and look to them for guidance. This requires true dedication and effort on the part of both the colored and white believers. They each have much to learn and much to overcome, as you both so clearly realize.
On behalf of Shoghi Effendi, to individual believers, 3/17/43

22. Do not for a moment hesitate or slacken in your efforts for such a glorious cause—and encourage the friends to exemplify the harmony and good will that should characterize the relations of races to one another, before attempting to summon the multitude to its urgent call. Let them search their own hearts, purge their own minds before attempting the regeneration of mankind.
Shoghi Effendi, to an individual believer, 9/11/27

23. . . . [Shoghi Effendi] feels that the friends should constantly be encouraged to bear in mind certain salient facts: Bahá'u'lláh has brought a new system and new laws and standards of personal as well as racial conduct into the world. Although outside agencies have been to a certain extent illumined by the radiance of His message and doctrines, and are exerting efforts to bring the world into that orbit of universal peace and harmony He has set for it, these outside

forces cannot achieve what only the followers of His Faith can. The believers must not take their eyes off their own immediate tasks of patiently consolidating their administrative institutions, building up new Assemblies ... and laboring to perfect the Bahá'í pattern of life, for these are things that no other group of people in the world can do or will do, and they alone are able to provide the spiritual foundation and example on which the larger world schemes must ultimately rest. At the same time every effort should be made to broadcast the Teachings at this time, and correlate them to the plight of humanity and the plans for its future.
    Shoghi Effendi, *Principles of Bahá'í Administration*, p. 87

24. The Bahá'ís are the leaven of God, which must leaven the lump of their nation. In direct ratio to their success will be the protection vouchsafed, not only to them but to their country. These are the immutable laws of God, from which there is no escape: "For unto whomsoever much is given, of him shall be much required."
    On behalf of Shoghi Effendi, *The Individual and Teaching*, p. 40

25. Every other consideration should be sacrificed for the sake of unity in the body of the Cause—a unity that can be achieved only when the Assemblies are helped and obeyed.
    On behalf of Shoghi Effendi, to an individual believer, 3/29/32

26. The blessings of the Ancient Beauty are being showered upon the followers of the Greatest Name. Our efforts to serve Him and humanity are being crowned with victories throughout the world. As we give thanks for these splendid achievements, as the Cause of God spreads in every land, as our institutions become more perfected, as the number of believers increases over the face of the planet, our individual lives must increasingly mirror forth each day the teachings of Bahá'u'lláh and we must so live our lives that all will see in us a different people. The acts we perform, the attitudes we

manifest, the very words we speak should be an attraction, a magnet, drawing the sincere to the Divine Teachings.

Bahá'u'lláh tells us that prejudice in its various forms destroys the edifice of humanity. We are adjured by the Divine Messenger to eliminate all forms of prejudice from our lives. Our outer lives must show forth our beliefs. The world must see that, regardless of each passing whim or current fashion of the generality of mankind, the Bahá'í lives his life according to the tenets of his Faith. We must not allow the fear of rejection by our friends and neighbors to deter us from our goal: to live the Bahá'í life. Let us strive to blot out from our lives every last trace of prejudice—racial, religious, political, economic, national, tribal, class, cultural, and that which is based on differences of education or age. We shall be distinguished from our non-Bahá'í associates if our lives are adorned with this principle.

If we allow prejudice of any kind to manifest itself in us, we shall be guilty before God of causing a setback to the progress and real growth of the Faith of Bahá'u'lláh. It is incumbent upon every believer to endeavor with a fierce determination to eliminate this defect from his thoughts and acts. It is the duty of the institutions of the Faith to inculcate this principle in the hearts of the friends through every means at their disposal including summer schools, conferences, institutes and study classes.

The fundamental purpose of the Faith of Bahá'u'lláh is the realization of the organic unity of the entire human race. Bearing this glorious destiny in mind, and with entire reliance on the promises of the Blessed Beauty, we should follow His exhortation:

"We love to see you at all times consorting in amity and concord within the paradise of My good-pleasure, and to inhale from your acts the fragrance of friendliness and unity, of loving kindness and fellowship."

The Universal House of Justice, *Messages from the Universal House of Justice*, pp. 99–100

27. With regard to the question of what public role might be played by the Bahá'í Faith in America to ameliorate in the immediately foreseeable future the plight of African-American males, the size and influence of the Bahá'í community are, alas, too limited for it to have a determining impact on conditions which have, after all, been hundreds of years in the making. As is well known, since at least the middle of the last century significant numbers of Americans, both black and white, have long labored, often with immense resourcefulness, to counteract the baleful legacy of racism in their country, in all its complex dimensions, structural and otherwise. Indeed, when one meditates on the sweep of United States history, one can see how unlikely it is that the bitter predicament of black males will be quickly or easily resolved. The obstacles are not of such character that, for example, legal reforms could dissolve them. This is not a counsel of despair. Nor is it to say an equivocation or a suggestion that the requirements of divine justice ought to be deferred. Nor is it to say that Bahá'ís have no critical role to play. On the contrary, the concern is with Bahá'í fundamentals, with looking deeply into underlying causes and identifying strategic lines of action which make the wisest use of our limited resources at this point in the development of the Bahá'í community.

If we are to avoid becoming entrammeled in the enervating coils of cynicism which are a characteristic of this age of transition, we must, as the "custodians of . . . the forces of love", ground our efforts in indomitable faith. In the future the Cause of God will spread throughout America; millions will be enlisted under its banner and race prejudice will finally be exorcised from the body politic. Of this have no doubt. It is inexorable, because it is the Will of Almighty God. However, as the House of Justice has been trying to get the friends to understand for some time, the necessary precondition to translation of our community's social vision into reality is a massive expansion in the number of committed, deepened believers who are well-grounded in the essentials of the Cause. Those who fail to comprehend the urgency assigned to the objective of achieving a large expansion have obviously failed to appreciate the moral imperative behind this aim.

Parallel to the process of large-scale enrollment, the institutions of the Faith, including those at the grassroots of the community, will gradually come to function with greater efficiency and increasing harmony, thereby enhancing their potential in stimulating the processes of social development.

Concerning the comparison you have drawn in your letter between the situation of the Bahá'í community in Iran and the African-American people generally, it is noteworthy that, while the plight of the Iranian friends is grievous, it is also in some essential respects far more tractable. Furthermore, since the community is organized around the divine Teachings and empowered by the Word of God, the effects of victimization on the Iranian believers is likely to prove, in the long view, less devastating than the effects of that which has been inflicted upon the African-Americans. Moreover, it is wholly conceivable that a tiny handful of secular and clerical rulers who control the government there could, more or less at the stroke of a pen, effectively emancipate that community from the bulk of its practical difficulties. Nonetheless, we are the only ones in the world who would so persistently direct the focus of international attention toward achieving the aim of lifting the shackles from our co-religionists. There is no one else to take the lead.

The House of Justice sympathizes with your frustrations. It feels, however, that the best contribution which the friends can make is to carry on with work of the kind you are already doing, demonstrating the Bahá'í spirit to others, showing their love for mankind and patiently, determinedly working to bring about a change in the hearts and minds of those they are able to reach. It is a question of being in this struggle for the long term, of advancing the issue as much as feasible, given the conditions with which one has to work. In this respect, the powerful example of the Hand of the Cause Louis Gregory is an invaluable source of inspiration and encouragement....

Your sedulous efforts to effect greater understanding, unity and love between the races are praiseworthy and will undoubtedly attract divine confirmations. Be assured of the continued prayers of the House of Justice at the Sacred Threshold that your efforts may yield fruit.
On behalf of the Universal House of Justice, to an individual believer, 4/1/96

II. Responsibilities of the Bahá'ís of European Descent

Let the white make a supreme effort in their resolve
to contribute their share to the solution of this problem,
to abandon once for all their usually inherent and
at times subconscious sense of superiority,
to correct their tendency towards revealing a patronizing attitude
towards the members of the other race,
to persuade them through their intimate, spontaneous and
informal association with them of the genuineness
of their friendship and the sincerity of their intentions,
and to master their impatience of any lack of responsiveness
on the part of a people who have received, for so long a period,
such grievous and slow-healing wounds.
Shoghi Effendi

28. And amongst the realms of unity is the unity of rank and station. It redoundeth to the exaltation of the Cause, glorifying it among all peoples. Ever since the seeking of preference and distinction came into play, the world hath been laid waste. It hath become desolate. Those who have quaffed from the ocean of divine utterance and fixed their gaze upon the Realm of Glory should regard themselves as being on the same level as the others and in the same station. Were this matter to be definitely established and conclusively demonstrated through the power and might of God, the world would become as the Abhá Paradise.

Indeed, man is noble, inasmuch as each one is a repository of the sign of God. Nevertheless, to regard oneself as superior in knowledge, learning or virtue, or to exalt oneself or seek preference, is a grievous transgression.
Bahá'u'lláh, in The Continental Boards of Counsellors, pp. 59–60

29. I pray that you attain to such a degree of good character and behavior that the names of black and white shall vanish. All shall be called human, just as the name for a flight of doves is dove. They are not called black and white. Likewise with other birds.

I hope that you attain to such a high degree—and this is impossible except through love. You must try to create love between yourselves; and this love does not come about unless you are grateful to the whites, and the whites are loving toward you, and endeavor to promote your advancement and enhance your honor. This will be the cause of love. Differences between black and white will be completely obliterated; indeed, ethnic and national differences will all disappear.

I am very happy to see you and thank God that this meeting is composed of people of both races and that both are gathered in perfect love and harmony. I hope this becomes the example of universal harmony and love until no title remains except that of humanity. Such a title demonstrates

the perfection of the human world and is the cause of eternal glory and human happiness. I pray that you be with one another in utmost harmony and love and strive to enable each other to live in comfort.
> 'Abdu'l-Bahá, presentation at Howard University, 4/23/12,
> *The Promulgation of Universal Peace*, pp. 44–46

30. No less serious is the stress and strain imposed on the fabric of American society through the fundamental and persistent neglect, by the governed and governors alike, of the supreme, the inescapable and urgent duty—so repeatedly and graphically represented and stressed by 'Abdu'l-Bahá in His arraignment of the basic weaknesses in the social fabric of the nation—of remedying, while there is yet time, through a revolutionary change in the concept and attitude of the average white American toward his Negro fellow citizen, a situation which, if allowed to drift, will, in the words of 'Abdu'l-Bahá, cause the streets of American cities to run with blood, aggravating thereby the havoc which the fearful weapons of destruction, raining from the air, and amassed by a ruthless, a vigilant, a powerful and inveterate enemy, will wreak upon those same cities.
> Shoghi Effendi, *Citadel of Faith*, pp. 126–27

31. Let the white make a supreme effort in their resolve to contribute their share to the solution of this problem, to abandon once for all their usually inherent and at times subconscious sense of superiority, to correct their tendency towards revealing a patronizing attitude towards the members of the other race, to persuade them through their intimate, spontaneous and informal association with them of the genuineness of their friendship and the sincerity of their intentions, and to master their impatience of any lack of responsiveness on the part of a people who have received, for so long a period, such grievous and slow-healing wounds.
> Shoghi Effendi, *The Advent of Divine Justice*, p. 33

32. "I hope," He ['Abdu'l-Bahá] thus addresses members of the white race, "that ye may cause that downtrodden race to become glorious, and to be joined with the white race, to serve the world of man with the utmost sincerity, faithfulness, love, and purity. This opposition, enmity, and prejudice among the white race and the colored cannot be effaced except through faith, assurance, and the teachings of the Blessed Beauty." "This question of the union of the white and the black is very important," He warns, "for if it is not realized, erelong great difficulties will arise, and harmful results will follow." "If this matter remaineth without change," is yet another warning, "enmity will be increased day by day, and the final result will be hardship and may end in bloodshed."
    Shoghi Effendi, quoting 'Abdu'l-Bahá in *The Advent of Divine Justice*, p. 33

33. White American Bahá'ís, he feels, although they have very much less prejudice than the American people, are nevertheless tainted to some extent with this national evil, perhaps wholly unconsciously so. Therefore, it behooves every believer of white extraction to carefully study his own attitude, and to see whether he is condescending in his relations with his fellow-Bahá'ís of Negro extraction, whether he ever unconsciously insults them by using the term "nigger" or being patronizingly kind, whether he invites them freely to his home, and makes friends of them to such a point that he no longer knows whether they are colored or white, but only thinks of them as Bill or Mary, so to speak.
    On behalf of Shoghi Effendi, to the Bahá'í Inter-Racial Teaching Committee, 5/27/57

34. Redouble your efforts in connection with the promotion of interracial amity and understanding. Urge the believers to show more affection, confidence, fellowship and loving kindness to the colored believers. No trace of mistrust, no sense of superiority, no mark of discord and aloofness should charac-

terize the relations of the white and colored believers. They should openly, bravely and sincerely follow the example of our Beloved and banish prejudice from their hearts. May He reinforce and bless your efforts in such an important field of work.
Shoghi Effendi, *Bahá'í News*, no. 18, 6/27, p. 5

35. Every believer, without any distinction, has his own part in the Divine Plan established by Bahá'u'lláh. Every one has his duties and responsibilities, and those are commensurate with his gifts and capacities. Let the friends therefore banish from their hearts every feeling of superiority complex. They are all but servants unto Him.
On behalf of Shoghi Effendi, to individual believers, 12/20/36

36. Nothing will so deeply affect the hearts of people who have been hurt and offended by the attitude of white supremacy as to consort with them as full equals—as indeed they are. . . .
On behalf of Shoghi Effendi, *The Power of Unity*, p. 77

37. The Negroes, likewise, are, one might say, a key problem and epitomize the feelings of color prejudice so rife in the United States. That is why he has so constantly emphasized the importance of the Bahá'ís actively and continuously demonstrating that in the Faith this cruel and horrible taint of discrimination against, and contempt for, them does not exist but on the contrary is supplanted by a feeling of esteem for their great gifts and a complete lack of prejudice in every field of life.
On behalf of Shoghi Effendi, *Bahá'í News*, no. 188, 10/46, pp. 3–4

38. A tremendous effort is required by both races if their outlook, their manners, and conduct are to reflect, in this darkened age, the spirit and teachings of the Faith of Bahá'u'lláh. Casting away once and for all the fallacious doctrine of racial superiority, with all its attendant evils,

confusion, and miseries, and welcoming and encouraging the intermixture of races, and tearing down the barriers that now divide them, they should each endeavor, day and night, to fulfill their particular responsibilities in the common task which so urgently faces them.
Shoghi Effendi, *The Advent of Divine Justice*, p. 33

39. Whether colored or noncolored, neither race has the right, or can conscientiously claim, to be regarded as absolved from such an obligation, as having realized such hopes, or having faithfully followed such an example. A long and thorny road, beset with pitfalls, still remains untraveled, both by the white and the Negro exponents of the redeeming Faith of Bahá'u'lláh.
Shoghi Effendi, *The Advent of Divine Justice*, pp. 28–29

40. Strive earnestly and put forth your greatest endeavor toward the accomplishment of this fellowship and the cementing of this bond of brotherhood between you. Such an attainment is not possible without will and effort on the part of each; from one, expressions of gratitude and appreciation; from the other, kindliness and recognition of equality. Each one should endeavor to develop and assist the other toward mutual advancement. . . .
'Abdu'l-Bahá, in *The Advent of Divine Justice*, pp. 32–33

41. Let neither think that the solution of so vast a problem is a matter that exclusively concerns the other. Let neither think that such a problem can either easily or immediately be resolved. Let neither think that they can wait confidently for the solution of this problem until the initiative has been taken, and the favorable circumstances created, by agencies that stand outside the orbit of their Faith. Let neither think that anything short of genuine love, extreme patience, true humility, consummate tact, sound initiative, mature wisdom, and deliberate, persistent, and prayerful effort, can

succeed in blotting out the stain which this patent evil has left on the fair name of their common country. Let them rather believe, and be firmly convinced, that on their mutual understanding, their amity, and sustained cooperation, must depend, more than on any other force or organization operating outside the circle of their Faith, the deflection of that dangerous course so greatly feared by 'Abdu'l-Bahá, and the materialization of the hopes He cherished for their joint contribution to the fulfillment of that country's glorious destiny.

Shoghi Effendi, *The Advent of Divine Justice*, p. 34

III. Responsibilities of the Bahá'ís of African Descent

*The Guardian feels very strongly
that the Negro Bahá'ís have great responsibilities,
both towards their own race and towards their fellow-believers.
They must not only arise to teach the Cause
to the members of their own race,
but must do all in their power to ensure that
within their Bahá'í Community itself
the Negro and white believers understand and love each other
and are truly as one soul in different bodies.*
Shoghi Effendi

42. I hope that thou mayest become a herald of the Kingdom and a means whereby the white and colored people shall close their eyes to racial differences and behold the reality of humanity, which is the universal unity. In other words, it is the oneness and wholeness of the human race, and the manifestation of the bounty of the Almighty. Look not upon thy frailty and thy limited capacity; look thou upon the Bounties and Providence of the Lord of the Kingdom, for His Confirmation is great, and His Power unparalleled and incomparable. Rely as much as thou canst upon the True One, and be thou resigned to the Will of God, so that like unto

a candle thou mayest be enkindled in the world of humanity and like unto a star thou mayest shine and gleam from the Horizon of Reality and become the cause of the guidance of both races.
> 'Abdu'l-Bahá, Tablet to Louis Gregory, *The Power of Unity*, p. 66

43. Today I am most happy, for I see here a gathering of the servants of God. I see white and black sitting together. There are no whites and blacks before God. All colors are one, and that is the color of servitude to God. Scent and color are not important. The heart is important. If the heart is pure, white or black or any color makes no difference. God does not look at colors; He looks at the hearts. He whose heart is pure is better. He whose character is better is more pleasing. He who turns more to the Abhá Kingdom is more advanced.

In the realm of existence colors are of no importance. Observe in the mineral kingdom colors are not the cause of discord. In the vegetable kingdom the colors of multicolored flowers are not the cause of discord. Rather, colors are the cause of the adornment of the garden because a single color has no appeal; but when you observe many-colored flowers, there is charm and display.

The world of humanity, too, is like a garden, and humankind are like the many-colored flowers. Therefore, different colors constitute an adornment. In the same way, there are many colors in the realm of animals. Doves are of many colors; nevertheless, they live in utmost harmony. They never look at color; instead, they look at the species. How often white doves fly with black ones. In the same way, other birds and varicolored animals never look at color; they look at the species.

Now ponder this: Animals, despite the fact that they lack reason and understanding, do not make colors the cause of conflict. Why should man, who has reason, create conflict? This is wholly unworthy of him. Especially white and black are the descendants of the same Adam; they belong to one household. In origin they were one; they were the same color. Adam was of one color. Eve had one color. All humanity is descended from them. Therefore, in origin they are one. These colors developed later due to climates and regions; they have no significance whatsoever. Therefore, today I am very happy that white and black have gathered together in this meeting. I hope this coming together and harmony reaches such a degree that no distinctions shall remain between them, and they shall be together in the utmost harmony and love.

But I wish to say one thing in order that the blacks may become grateful to the whites and the whites become loving toward the blacks. If you go to Africa and see the blacks of Africa, you will realize how much progress you have made. Praise be to God! You are like the whites; there are no great distinctions left. But the blacks of Africa are treated as servants. The first proclamation of emancipation for the blacks was made by the whites of America. How they fought and sacrificed until they freed the blacks! Then it spread to other places. The blacks of Africa were in complete bondage, but your emancipation led to their freedom also—that is, the European states emulated the Americans, and the emancipation proclamation became universal. It was for your sake that the whites of America made such an effort. Were it not for this effort, universal emancipation would not have been proclaimed.

Therefore, you must be very grateful to the whites of America, and the whites must become very loving toward you so that you may progress in all human grades. Strive jointly to make extraordinary progress and mix together completely. In short, you must be very thankful to the whites who were the cause of your freedom in America. Had you not been freed, other blacks would not have been freed either. Now—praise be to God!—everyone is free and lives in tranquility. I pray that you attain to such a degree of good character and behavior that the names of black and white shall vanish. All shall be called human, just as the name for a flight of doves is dove. They are not called black and white. Likewise with other birds.

I hope that you attain to such a high degree—and this is impossible except through love. You must try to create love between yourselves; and this love does not come about unless you are grateful to the whites, and the whites are loving toward you, and endeavor to promote your advancement and enhance your honor. This will be the cause of love. Differences between black and white will be completely obliterated; indeed, ethnic and national differences will all disappear.

I am very happy to see you and thank God that this meeting is composed of people of both races and that both are gathered in perfect love and harmony. I hope this becomes the example of universal harmony and love until no title remains except that of humanity. Such a title demonstrates the perfection of the human world and is the cause of eternal glory and human happiness. I pray that you be with one another in utmost harmony and love and strive to enable each other to live in comfort.

> 'Abdu'l-Bahá, presentation at Howard University, 4/23/12, *The Promulgation of Universal Peace*, pp. 44–46

44. He [the Guardian] is well aware that the conditions within the ranks of the believers in respect to race prejudice [are] far from being as [they] should be. However, he feels very strongly that it presents a challenge to both white and colored believers.

As we neither feel nor acknowledge any distinction between the duties and privileges of a Bahá'í, whoever he may be, it is incumbent upon the Negro believers to rise above this great test which the attitude of some of their white brethren may present. They must prove their innate equality not by words but by deeds. They must accept the Cause of

Bahá'u'lláh for the sake of the Cause, love it, and cling to it, and teach it, and fight for it as their own Cause, forgetful of the shortcomings of others. Any other attitude is unworthy of their faith.

Proud and happy in the praises which even Bahá'u'lláh Himself has bestowed upon them, they must feel He revealed Himself for them and every other downtrodden race, loves them, and will help them to attain their destiny.

The whole race question in America is a national one and of great importance. But the Negro friends must not waste their precious opportunity to serve the Faith, in these momentous days, by dwelling on the admitted shortcomings of the white friends. They must arise and serve and teach, confident of the future they are building, a future in which we know these barriers will have once and for all been overcome! . . .

May the Beloved of our hearts guide and sustain you in your constant activities, enable you to increase the number of the colored believers, whose interests are close to my heart, and for whom I continually and ardently beseech the guidance and the blessings of Bahá'u'lláh.†
On behalf of Shoghi Effendi, 2/9/42

45. Let the Negroes, through a corresponding effort on their part, show by every means in their power the warmth of their response, their readiness to forget the past, and their ability to wipe out every trace of suspicion that may still linger in their hearts and minds.
Shoghi Effendi, *The Advent of Divine Justice*, pp. 33–34

46. Movements for social progress and racial justice, as long as they are disassociated from both political and religious

---

†The last paragraph was in the handwriting of Shoghi Effendi.

partisanship, should be supported by those Bahá'ís who feel urged to undertake such work. Consequently there is no reason why you should not work for the betterment of your race through channels that in no way conflict with our Bahá'í attitude.

However meritorious such work may be, we should, however, never lose sight of the fact that ultimately the only solution for the problems facing not only the Negro, but the entire human race, is that which Bahá'u'lláh has embodied in His teachings. The more various racial movements of reform make progress, the easier it will be for society to accept our enlightened teachings. But such movements can never alone solve the grave problems facing men today.

The Guardian feels very strongly that the Negro Bahá'ís have great responsibilities, both towards their own race and towards their fellow-believers. They must not only arise to teach the Cause to the members of their own race, but must do all in their power to ensure that within their Bahá'í Community itself the Negro and white believers understand and love each other and are truly as one soul in different bodies. Our allegiance as believers is to Bahá'u'lláh; we must fix our attention and devotion on Him, and His Will, and, heedless of the shortcomings of our fellow-Bahá'ís, act as He would have us towards them.

On behalf of Shoghi Effendi, to an individual believer, 11/23/41

47. He was very happy to hear of how active and devoted you and your family are in the service of the Faith—particularly to learn that you are of the Negro race, as it always rejoices his heart to receive news that the colored friends are assuming their full Bahá'í responsibilities, and demonstrating, in a country so tainted with race prejudice, the unity of the friends, of all races, in the Cause of God.

You may be sure he will pray for the unity of the . . . believers, as this is of paramount importance, and upon it depends the development of the Cause there, and the success of every teaching effort. The thing the friends need—everywhere—is a greater love for each other, and this can be acquired by greater love for Bahá'u'lláh, for if we love Him deeply enough, we will never allow personal feelings and opinions to hold His Cause back; we will be willing to sacrifice ourselves to each other for the sake of the Faith, and be, as the Master said, one soul in many bodies.

On behalf of Shoghi Effendi, to an individual believer, 9/6/46

48. The Universal House of Justice has received your letter ... discussing the many difficulties faced by people of color in America, with particular reference to the Bahá'í community....

Even if all you describe is so, you share in common with your fellow believers the unique bounty of having recognized the Supreme Manifestation of God, Bahá'u'lláh. This fact empowers you and them to engage in a necessary process of spiritual transformation, a process which is slow and sometimes can be painful. The most significant contribution one can make to the progress of such a transformation is first to deal with one's own spiritual deficiencies, then to attempt lovingly, patiently and confidently to encourage others in their strivings to adhere to the principles of the Cause. However, such encouragement is most effective not through words alone, but especially to the extent one's own "... inner life and private character mirror forth in their manifold aspects the splendor of those eternal principles proclaimed by Bahá'u'lláh".

Regarding relations between the races, in *The Advent of Divine Justice*, Shoghi Effendi has clearly indicated the attitude and actions which will enable the friends, black or white, to deal with this entrenched and seemingly intractable problem. You also may wish to read about the life of the Hand of the Cause Louis Gregory to see how 'Abdu'l-Bahá's unbounded love so transformed him that he in turn became a potent instrument in effecting transformation in others, enabling him to triumph over racial prejudice at one of the saddest and worst periods of racial discrimination in the history of the United States. Look with the eye of fairness at how much things have changed for the better since that time, and be confident that the example Mr. Gregory set, if followed, can effect greater changes than have already occurred.

There is no way in which one can retreat to one's ethnic circle and find peace by building a fence around it. The goal is unity. In this new period of human history when the earth with all its diversity of peoples has become a single neighborhood, each Bahá'í must resolutely face the challenge of achieving unity and making peace. The House of Justice has noted that the National Spiritual Assembly of the United States has initiated a race unity campaign, which it hopes will go far in removing the blight of race prejudice from the American people. It hopes that you will lend your cooperation and energy to this work, which has ramifications not only for the people of America but, potentially, for the planet as a whole.

Be assured of the ardent prayers of the House of Justice in the Holy Shrines that you may receive divine assistance as you arise to play your part in addressing the most vital and challenging issue facing the American community. . . .

The Universal House of Justice, to an individual believer, 9/2/92

IV. Reliance Upon Divine Power and the Love of God

*But there is need of a superior power
to overcome human prejudices,
a power which nothing in the world of mankind can withstand
and which will overshadow the effect
of all other forces at work in human conditions.
That irresistible power is the love of God.*
'Abdu'l-Bahá

*To bring the white and the black together
is consider impossible and unfeasible,
but the breaths of the Holy Spirit will bring about this union.*
'Abdu'l-Bahá

49. He, the divine King, hath proclaimed the undisputed supremacy of the verses of His Book over all things that testify to His truth. . . . Through them floweth the river of divine knowledge, and gloweth the fire of His ancient and consummate wisdom. This is the fire which, in one and the same moment, kindleth the flame of love in the breasts of the faithful, and induceth the chill of heedlessness in the heart of the enemy.
    Bahá'u'lláh, *The Kitab-i-Íqán*, p. 205

50. O people of Justice! Be as brilliant as the light, and as splendid as the fire that blazed in the Burning Bush. The brightness of the fire of your love will no doubt fuse and unify the contending peoples and kindreds of the earth, whilst the fierceness of the flame of enmity and hatred cannot but result in strife and ruin.
    Bahá'u'lláh, *Gleanings*, p. 96

51. If any differences arise amongst you, behold Me standing before your face, and overlook the faults of one another for My name's sake and as a token of your love for My manifest and resplendent Cause. We love to see you at all times consorting in amity and concord within the paradise of My good-pleasure, and to inhale from your acts the fragrance of friendliness and unity, of loving-kindness and fellowship...

  We shall always be with you; if We inhale the perfume of your fellowship, Our heart will assuredly rejoice, for naught else can satisfy Us.
    Bahá'u'lláh, *Gleanings*, pp. 315–16

52. By God besides Whom is none other God! Should any one arise for the triumph of our Cause, him will God render victorious though tens of thousands of enemies be leagued against him. And if his love for Me wax stronger, God will establish his ascendancy over all the powers of earth and heaven. Thus have We breathed the spirit of power into all regions.
    Bahá'u'lláh, in *The World Order of Bahá'u'lláh*, p. 106

53. But there is need of a superior power to overcome human prejudices, a power which nothing in the world of mankind can withstand and which will overshadow the effect of all other forces at work in human conditions. That irresistible power is the love of God. It is my hope and prayer that it may destroy the prejudice of this one point of distinction [racial color] between you [the colored and white races] and unite you all permanently under its hallowed protection.
 'Abdu'l-Bahá, *The Promulgation of Universal Peace*, p. 68

54. We must find a way of spreading love among the sons of humanity.

Love is unlimited, boundless, infinite! Material things are limited, circumscribed, finite. You cannot adequately express infinite love by limited means.

The perfect love needs an unselfish instrument, absolutely freed from fetters of every kind. The love of family is limited; the tie of blood relationship is not the strongest bond. Frequently members of the same family disagree, and even hate each other.

Patriotic love is finite; the love of one's country causing hatred of all others, is not perfect love! Compatriots also are not free from quarrels amongst themselves.

The love of race is limited; there is some union here, but that is insufficient. Love must be free from boundaries!

To love our own race may mean hatred of all others, and even people of the same race often dislike each other.

Political love also is much bound up with hatred of one party for another; this love is very limited and uncertain.

The love of community of interest in service is likewise fluctuating; frequently competitions arise, which lead to jealousy, and at length hatred replaces love.

A few years ago, Turkey and Italy had a friendly political understanding; now they are at war!

All these ties of love are imperfect. It is clear that limited material ties are insufficient to adequately express the universal love.

The great unselfish love for humanity is bounded by none of these imperfect, semi-selfish bonds; this is the one perfect love, possible to all mankind, and can only be achieved by the power of the Divine Spirit. No worldly power can accomplish the universal love.

Let all be united in this Divine power of love! Let all strive to grow in the light of the Sun of Truth, and reflecting this luminous love on all men, may their hearts become so united that they may dwell evermore in the radiance of the limitless love.

'Abdu'l-Bahá, *Paris Talks*, pp. 36–37

55. Do not despair! Work steadily. Sincerity and love will conquer hate. How many seemingly impossible events are coming to pass in these days! Set your faces steadily towards the Light of the World. Show love to all; "Love is the breath of the Holy Spirit in the heart of Man." Take courage! God never forsakes His children who strive and work and pray! Let your hearts be filled with the strenuous desire that tranquillity and harmony may encircle all this warring world. So will success crown your efforts, and with the universal brotherhood will come the Kingdom of God in peace and goodwill.

'Abdu'l-Bahá, *Paris Talks*, p. 30

56. And now you, if you act in accordance with the teachings of Bahá'u'lláh, may rest assured that you will be aided and confirmed. In all affairs which you undertake, you shall be rendered victorious, and all the inhabitants of the earth cannot withstand you. You are the conquerors, because the power of the Holy Spirit is your assistant. Above and over physical forces, phenomenal forces, the Holy Spirit itself shall aid you.

'Abdu'l-Bahá, in *Star of the West*, vol. 8, no. 8, p. 103

57. O ye my soldiers of the Kingdom!

. . . Be ye valiant and fearless! Day by day add to your

spiritual victories. Be ye not disturbed by the constant assaults of the enemies. Attack ye like unto the roaring lions. Have no thought of yourselves, for the invisible armies of the Kingdom are fighting on your side. Enter ye the battlefield with the Confirmations of the Holy Spirit. Know ye of a certainty that the powers of the Kingdom of Abhá are with you. The hosts of the heaven of Truth are with you. The cool breezes of the Paradise of Abhá are wafting over your heated brows. Not for a moment are ye alone. Not for a second are ye left to yourselves. The Beauty of Abhá is with you. The Glorious God is with you. The King of Kings is with you.
'Abdu'l-Bahá, in *Star of the West*, vol. 13, no. 5, p. 113

58. Bahá'u'lláh teaches that the world of humanity is in need of the breath of the Holy Spirit, for in spiritual quickening and enlightenment true oneness is attained with God and man. The Most Great Peace cannot be assured through racial force and effort. . . . Universal peace is an impossibility through human and material agencies; it must be through spiritual power. There is need of a universal impelling force which will establish the oneness of humanity and destroy the foundations of war and strife. None other than the divine power can do this; therefore, it will be accomplished through the breath of the Holy Spirit.
'Abdu'l-Bahá, *The Promulgation of Universal Peace*, pp. 108–09

59. To bring the white and the black together is consider impossible and unfeasible, but the breaths of the Holy Spirit will bring about this union.
. . . the enmity and hatred which exist between the white and the black races is very dangerous and there is no doubt that it will end in bloodshed unless the influence of the Word of God, the breaths of the Holy Spirit and the teachings of Bahá'u'lláh are diffused amóngst them and harmony is established between the two races.

They must destroy the foundation of enmity and rancor and lay the basis of love and affinity. The power of the Teachings of Bahá'u'lláh will remove this danger from America.
    'Abdu'l-Bahá, *The Power of Unity*, p. 31

60. The friends must realize the Power of the Holy Spirit which is manifest and quickening them at this time through the appearance of Bahá'u'lláh. There is no force of heaven or earth which can affect them if they place themselves wholly under the influence of the Holy Spirit and under its guidance.
    On behalf of Shoghi Effendi, *The Power of Divine Assistance*, pp. 56–57

61. ... the Holy Spirit is like unto the life in the human body, which blends all differences of parts and members in unity and agreement. ... Just as the human spirit of life is the cause of coordination among the various parts of the human organism, the Holy Spirit is the controlling cause of the unity and coordination of mankind. That is to say, the bond or oneness of humanity cannot be effectively established save through the power of the Holy Spirit, for the world of humanity is a composite body, and the Holy Spirit is the animating principle of its life.
    'Abdu'l-Bahá, *The Promulgation of Universal Peace*, p. 321

62. Therefore we have need of a general power which may dominate the sentiments, the opinions, and the thoughts of all, thanks to which these divisions may no longer have effect, and all individuals may be brought under the influence of the unity of the world of humanity. It is clear and evident that this greatest power in the human world is the love of God. It brings the different peoples under the shadow of the tent of affection; it gives to the antagonistic and hostile nations and families the greatest love and union.
    'Abdu'l-Bahá, *Some Answered Questions*, pp. 345–46

63. Love is the fundamental principle of God's purpose for man, and He has commanded us to love each other even as He loves us.
    'Abdu'l-Bahá, *Paris Talks*, p. 122

64. Unity is love. It cannot be established without love.
    'Abdu'l-Bahá, *Star of the West*, vol. VIII, no. 10, p. 121

65. In the world of existence there is indeed no greater power than the power of love. . . .
    There are four kinds of love. The first is the love that flows from God to man. . . . This love is the origin of all the love in the world of creation.
    The second is the love that flows from man to God. . . . This love is the origin of all philanthropy; this love causes the hearts of men to reflect the rays of the Sun of Reality.
    The third is the love of God towards the Self or Identity of God. . . . Through one ray of this Love all other love exists.
    The fourth is the love of man for man. The love which exists between the hearts of believers is prompted by the ideal of the unity of spirits. This love is attained through the knowledge of God, so that men see the Divine Love reflected in the heart. Each sees in the other the Beauty of God reflected in the soul, and finding this point of similarity, they are attracted to one another in love. This love will make all men the waves of one sea, this love will make them all the stars of one heaven and the fruits of one tree. This love will bring the realization of true accord, the foundation of real unity.
    'Abdu'l-Bahá, *Paris Talks*, pp. 179–81

66. This means the oneness of the world of humanity. That is to say, when this human body-politic reaches a state of absolute unity, the effulgence of the eternal Sun will make its fullest light and heat manifest. Therefore we must not make distinctions between individual members of the human family. We must not consider any soul as barren or deprived. Our

duty lies in educating souls so that the Sun of the bestowals of God shall become resplendent in them, and this is possible through the power of the oneness of humanity. The more love is expressed among mankind and the stronger the power of unity, the greater will be this reflection and revelation, for the greatest bestowal of God is love. Love is the source of all the bestowals of God. Until love takes possession of the heart no other divine bounty can be revealed in it.
    'Abdu'l-Bahá, *Bahá'í World Faith*, p. 218

67. Should one soul from amongst the believers meet another, it must be as though a thirsty one with parched lips has reached to the fountain of the water of life, or a lover has met his true beloved. For one of the greatest divine wisdoms regarding the appearance of the Holy Manifestations is this: The souls may come to know each other and become intimate with each other; the power of the love of God may make all of them the waves of one sea, the flowers of one rose garden, and the stars of one heaven.
    'Abdu'l-Bahá, *Tablets of the Divine Plan*, p. 50

68. . . . when any souls grow to be true believers, they will attain a spiritual relationship with one another, and show forth a tenderness which is not of this world. They will, all of them, become elated from a draught of divine love, and that union of theirs, that connection, will also abide forever. Souls, that is, who will consign their own selves to oblivion, strip from themselves the defects of humankind, and unchain themselves from human bondage, will beyond any doubt be illumined with the heavenly splendors of oneness, and will all attain unto real union in the world that dieth not.
    'Abdu'l-Bahá, *Selections from the Writings of 'Abdu'l-Bahá*, pp. 117–18

69. We must love God, and in this state, a general love for all men becomes possible. We cannot love each human being for

himself, but our feeling towards humanity should be motivated by our love for the Father who created all men.
        Shoghi Effendi, *Living the Life*, p. 32

70. We must become entirely selfless and devoted to God so that every day and every moment we seek to do only what God would have us do and in the way He would have us do it. If we do this sincerely then we shall have perfect unity and harmony with each other. Where there is want of harmony, there is lack of the true Bahá'í Spirit. Unless we can show this transformation in our lives, this new power, this mutual love and harmony, then the Bahá'í teachings are but a name to us.
        On behalf of Shoghi Effendi, *Living the Life*, p. 9

71. The thing the friends need—everywhere—is a greater love for each other, and this can be acquired by greater love for Bahá'u'lláh; for if we love Him deeply enough, we will never allow personal feelings and opinions to hold His Cause back; we will be willing to sacrifice ourselves to each other for the sake of the Faith, and be, as the Master said, one soul in many bodies.
        On behalf of Shoghi Effendi, *Living the Life*, p. 25

72. A greater degree of love will produce a greater unity, because it enables people to bear with each other, to be patient and forgiving.
        Shoghi Effendi, *Living the Life*, p. 21

73. In this wondrous Age . . . the Word of God hath infused such awesome power into the inmost essence of humankind that He hath stripped men's human qualities of all effect, and hath, with his all-conquering might, unified the peoples in a vast sea of oneness.
        'Abdu'l-Bahá, *Selections from the Writings of 'Abdu'l-Bahá*, p. 20

74. Naught but the celestial potency of the Word of God, which ruleth and transcendeth the realities of all things, is capable of harmonizing the divergent thoughts, sentiments,

ideas, and convictions of the children of men. Verily, it is the penetrating power in all things, the mover of souls and the binder and regulator in the world of humanity.
    'Abdu'l-Bahá, *Selection from the Writings of 'Abdu'l-Bahá*, p. 292

75. Today nothing but the power of the Divine Word, which embraces the Reality of all things, can draw together the minds, hearts, and spirits of the world under the shadow of the heavenly Tree of Unity.
    'Abdu'l-Bahá, *Star of the West*, vol. II, no. 9, p. 5

76. The friends need only read the Writings; the answers are all in them. . . .
    On behalf of Shoghi Effendi, *The Importance of Deepening*, p. 53

77. Indeed if an avowed follower of Bahá'u'lláh were to immerse himself in, and fathom the depths of, the ocean of these heavenly teachings, and with utmost care and attention deduce from each of them the subtle mysteries and consummate wisdom that lie enshrined therein, such a person's life, materially, intellectually and spiritually, will be safe from toil and trouble, and unaffected by setbacks and perils, or any sadness or despondency.
    Shoghi Effendi, *The Importance of Deepening*, p. 20

78. Consider to what extent the friends of God have been urged and exhorted in the Will and Testament as well as in the holy Tablets and Writings to show forth uprightness, good will, tolerance, sanctity, detachment from all things besides God, and severance from whatever pertains to this world, and to exemplify heavenly qualities and traits. First and foremost one should resort to every possible means to purge one's heart and motives, otherwise it would be futile to engage in any form of enterprise. It is also essential to abstain from hypocrisy and blind imitation, inasmuch as their foul odor would soon be detected by every man of understanding and wisdom. Moreover the friends must

observe the specific times for the remembrance of God, meditation, devotion and prayer, as it is highly unlikely, nay, rather impossible, that any enterprise should prosper and develop short of divine bestowals and confirmation. One can hardly imagine what a great influence genuine love, truthfulness and purity of motives exert on the souls of men. But these traits cannot be acquired unless every believer makes a daily effort to gain them. . . .
    Shoghi Effendi, *Living the Life*, pp. 7–8

79. The friends must, at all times, bear in mind that they are, in a way, like soldiers under attack. The world is at present in an exceedingly dark condition spiritually; hatred and prejudice of every sort, are literally tearing it to pieces. We, on the other hand, are the custodians of the opposite forces, the forces of love, of unity, of peace and integration, and we must constantly be on our guard, whether as individuals or as an assembly or community, lest through us these destructive, negative forces enter into our midst. In other words, we must beware lest the darkness of society become reflected in our acts and attitudes, perhaps all unconsciously. Love for each other, the deep sense that we are a new organism, the dawn-breakers of a New World Order, must constantly animate our Bahá'í lives, and we must pray to be protected from the contamination of society which is so diseased with prejudice.
    Shoghi Effendi, *Bahá'í News*, no. 210, 8/48, p. 2

80. Delicate and strenuous though the task may be, however arduous and prolonged the effort required, whatsoever the nature of the perils and pitfalls that beset the path of whoever arises to revive the fortunes of a Faith struggling against the rising forces of materialism, nationalism, secularism, racialism, ecclesiasticism, the all-conquering potency of the grace of God, vouchsafed through the Revelation of Bahá'u'lláh,

will, undoubtedly, mysteriously and surprisingly, enable whosoever arises to champion His Cause to win complete and total victory.
    Shoghi Effendi, *Citadel of Faith*, p. 149

V. The Standard of Faith During Tests and Adversities

As ye have faith
so shall your powers and blessings be.
'Abdu'l-Bahá

One soul can be the cause
of the spiritual illumination of a continent.
Shoghi Effendi

81. "Say: Beware, O people of Bahá, lest the strong ones of the earth rob you of your strength, or they who rule the world fill you with fear. Put your trust in God, and commit your affairs to His keeping. He, verily, will, through the power of truth, render you victorious, and He, verily, is powerful to do what He willeth, and in His grasp are the reins of omnipotent might." "I swear by My life! Nothing save that which profiteth them can befall My loved ones. To this testifieth the Pen of God, the Most Powerful, the All-Glorious, the Best Beloved." "Let not the happenings of the world sadden you. I swear by God! The sea of joy yearneth to attain your presence, for every good thing hath been created for you, and will, according to the needs of the times, be revealed unto you."
    Bahá'u'lláh, in *The Advent of Divine Justice*, p. 69

82. He will never deal unjustly with any one, neither will He task a soul beyond its power. He, verily, is the Compassionate, the All-Merciful.
    Bahá'u'lláh, *Gleanings*, p. 106

83. Regard not the all-sufficing power of God as an idle fancy. It is that genuine faith which thou cherishest for the Manifestation of God in every Dispensation. It is such faith which sufficeth above all the things that exist on the earth, whereas no created thing on earth besides faith would suffice thee. If thou art not a believer, the Tree of divine Truth would condemn thee to extinction. If thou art a believer, thy faith shall be sufficient for thee above all things that exist on earth, even though thou possess nothing.
   The Báb, *Selections from the Writings of the Báb*, p. 123

84. The tests of every dispensation are in direct proportion with the greatness of the Cause and as heretofore such a manifest Covenant, written by the Supreme Pen, has not been entered upon, the tests are proportionately severe.
   'Abdu'l-Bahá, *Star of the West*, vol. X, no. 14, p. 265

85. The world of humanity is filled with darkness; you are its radiant candles. It is very poor; you must be the treasury of the Kingdom. It is exceedingly debased; you must be the cause of its exaltation. It is bereft of divine graces; you must give it impetus and spiritual quickening. According to the teachings of Bahá'u'lláh you must love and cherish each individual member of humanity.
   The first sign of faith is love.
   'Abdu'l-Bahá, *The Promulgation of Universal Peace*, p. 337

86. Wherefore must the friends of God, with utter sanctity, with one accord, rise up in the spirit, in unity with one another, to such a degree that they will become even as one being and one soul. On such a plane as this, physical bodies play no part, rather doth the spirit take over and rule; and when its power encompasseth all then is spiritual union achieved. Strive ye by day and night to cultivate your unity to the fullest degree. Let your thoughts dwell on your own

spiritual development, and close your eyes to the deficiencies of other souls. Act ye in such wise, showing forth pure and goodly deeds, and modesty and humility, that ye will cause others to be awakened.

Never is it the wish of 'Abdu'l-Bahá to see any being hurt, nor will He make anyone to grieve; for man can receive no greater gift than this, that he rejoice another's heart. I beg of God that ye will be bringers of joy, even as are the angels in Heaven.
  'Abdu'l-Bahá, *Selections from the Writings of 'Abdu'l-Bahá*,
  pp. 203–04

87. ... I say unto you that anyone who will rise up in the Cause of God at this time shall be filled with the spirit of God, and that He will send His hosts from heaven to help you, and that nothing shall be impossible to you if you have faith. And now I give you a commandment which shall be for a covenant between you and Me—that ye have faith; that your faith be steadfast as a rock that no storms can move, that nothing can disturb, and that it endure through all things even to the end; even should ye hear that your Lord has been crucified, be not shaken in your faith; for I am with you always, whether living or dead, I am with you to the end. As ye have faith so shall your powers and blessings be. This is the balance—this is the balance—this is the balance.
  'Abdu'l-Bahá, *An Early Pilgrimage*, p. 40

88. As 'Abdu'l-Bahá said, nothing is impossible if we have faith; and this must always be the standard for all the Bahá'ís. As we have faith, so are our powers and our blessings.
  On behalf of Shoghi Effendi, *Dawn of a New Day*, p. 160

89. Is not faith but another word for implicit obedience, wholehearted allegiance, uncompromising adherence to that which we believe is the revealed and express will of God,

however perplexing it might first appear, however at variance with the shadowy views, the impotent doctrines, the crude theories, the idle imaginings, the fashionable conceptions of a transient and troublous age?
Shoghi Effendi, *Bahá'í Administration*, pp. 62–63

90. Just one mature soul, with spiritual understanding and a profound knowledge of the Faith, can set a whole country ablaze—so great is the power of the Cause to work through a pure and selfless channel.
On behalf of Shoghi Effendi, *The Power of Divine Assistance*, p. 55

91. This challenge, so severe and insistent, and yet so glorious, faces no doubt primarily the individual believer on whom, in the last resort, depends the fate of the entire community.
Shoghi Effendi, *Citadel of Faith*, pp. 130–31

92. Ultimately all the battle of life is within the individual. No amount of organization can solve the inner problems or produce or prevent, as the case may be, victory or failure at a crucial moment. In such times as these particularly, individuals are torn by great forces at large in the world, and we see some weak ones suddenly become miraculously strong, and strong ones fail—we can only try, through loving advice ... to bring about the act on the part of the believer which will be for the highest good of the Cause. Because obviously something bad for the Cause cannot be the highest good of the individual Bahá'í.
On behalf of Shoghi Effendi, *Living the Life*, p. 20

93. Human frailties and peculiarities can be a great test. But the only way, or perhaps I should say the first and best way, to remedy such situations, is to oneself do what is right. One soul can be the cause of the spiritual illumination of a

continent. Now that you have seen, and remedied, a great fault in your own life, now that you see more clearly what is lacking in your own community, there is nothing to prevent you from arising and showing such an example, such a love and spirit of service, as to enkindle the hearts of your fellow Bahá'ís.

He urges you to study deeply the teachings, teach others, study with those Bahá'ís who are anxious to do so, the deeper teachings of our Faith, and through example, effort and prayer, bring about a change.
On behalf of Shoghi Effendi, *The Ocean of My Words*, pp. 47–48

94. You have complained of the unsatisfactory conditions prevailing in the ... Bahá'í Community; the Guardian is well aware of the situation of the Cause there, but is confident that whatever the nature of the obstacles that confront the Faith they will be eventually overcome. You should, under no circumstances, feel discouraged, and allow such difficulties, even though they may have resulted from the misconduct, or the lack of capacity and vision of certain members of the Community, to make you waver in your faith and basic loyalty to the Cause. Surely, the believers, no matter how qualified they may be, whether as teachers or administrators, and however high their intellectual and spiritual merits, should never be looked upon as a standard whereby to evaluate and measure the divine authority and mission of the Faith. It is to the Teachings themselves, and to the lives of the Founders of the Cause that the believers should look for their guidance and inspiration, and only by keeping strictly to such true attitude can they hope to establish their loyalty to Bahá'u'lláh upon an enduring and unassailable basis. You should take heart, therefore, and with unrelaxing vigilance and unremitting effort endeavor to play your full share in the gradual unfoldment of this Divine World Order.
On behalf of Shoghi Effendi, *The Bahá'í Life*, p. 7

95. Often these trials and tests which all Bahá'í Communities inevitably pass through seem terrible, at the moment, but in retrospect we understand that they were due to the frailty of human nature, to misunderstandings, and to the growing pains which every Bahá'í Community must experience.
On behalf of Shoghi Effendi, *Living the Life*, p. 37

96. We must never dwell too much on the attitudes and feelings of our fellow-believers towards us. What is most important is to foster love and harmony and ignore any rebuffs we may receive; in this way the weaknesses of human nature and the peculiarity or attitude of any particular person is not magnified, but pales into insignificance in comparison with our joint service to the Faith we all love.
On behalf of Shoghi Effendi, *Living the Life*, p. 29

97. The friends must be patient with each other and must realize that the Cause is still in its infancy and its institutions are not yet functioning perfectly. The greater the patience, the loving understanding and the forbearance the believers show towards each other and their shortcomings the greater will be the progress of the whole Bahá'í Community at large.

One of the greatest problems in the Cause is the relation of the believers to each other; for their immaturity (shared with the rest of humanity) and imperfections retard the work, create complications, and discourage each other. And yet we must put up with these things and try and combat them through love, patience, and forgiveness individually and proper administrative action collectively.
On behalf of Shoghi Effendi, quoted by The Universal House of Justice, 7/23/74

98. The greatest need it seems everywhere inside the Cause is to impress upon the friends the need for love among them. There is a tendency to mix up the functions of the Adminis-

tration and try to apply it in individual relationships, which is abortive, because the Assembly is a nascent House of Justice and is supposed to administer, according to the Teachings, the affairs of the community. But individuals toward each other are governed by love, unity, forgiveness and a sin-covering eye. Once the friends grasp this they will get along much better, but they keep playing Spiritual Assembly to each other and expect the Assembly to behave like an individual. . . .
    On behalf of Shoghi Effendi, *The Bahá'í Life*, pp. 18–19

99. He (the Guardian) like the Master before him, is so anxious to see the believers united in serving the Faith. If between the friends, true love, based on the love of God, could become manifest, the Cause would spread very rapidly. Love is the standard which must govern the conduct of one believer towards another. The administrative order does not change this, but unfortunately sometimes the friends confuse the two, and try to be a whole spiritual assembly to each other, with the discipline and justice and impartiality that body must show, instead of being forgiving, loving, and patient to each other as individuals.
    On behalf of Shoghi Effendi, *Bahá'í News*, no. 238, 12/50, p. 10

100. When a person becomes a Bahá'í, actually what takes place is that the seed of the spirit starts to grow in the human soul. This seed must be watered by the outpourings of the Holy Spirit. These gifts of the spirit are received through prayer, meditation, study of the Holy Utterances and service to the Cause of God. The fact of the matter is that service in the Cause is like the plough which ploughs the physical soil when seeds are sown. It is necessary that the soil be ploughed up, so that it can be enriched, and thus cause a stronger growth of the seed. In exactly the same way the evolution of the spirit takes place through ploughing up the soil of the

heart so that it is a constant reflection of the Holy Spirit. In this way the human spirit grows and develops by leaps and bounds.

Naturally there will be periods of distress and difficulty, and even severe tests; but if that person turns firmly towards the divine Manifestation, studies carefully His spiritual teachings and receives the blessings of the Holy Spirit, he will find that in reality these tests and difficulties have been the gifts of God to enable him to grow and develop.

Thus you might look upon your own difficulties in the path of service. They are the means of your spirit growing and developing. You will suddenly find that you have conquered many of the problems which upset you, and then you will wonder why they should have troubled you at all. An individual must centre his whole heart and mind on service to the Cause, in accordance with the high standards set by Bahá'u'lláh. When this is done, the Hosts of the Supreme Concourse will come to the assistance of the individual, and every difficulty and trial will gradually be overcome.

On behalf of Shoghi Effendi, *Living the Life*, pp. 35–36

101. In order to achieve this cordial unity one of the first essentials insisted on by Bahá'u'lláh and 'Abdu'l-Bahá is that we resist the natural tendency to let our attention dwell on the faults and failings of others rather than on our own. Each of us is responsible for one life only, and that is our own. Each of us is immeasurably far from being "perfect as our heavenly Father is perfect" and the task of perfecting our own life and character is one that requires all our attention, our willpower and energy. If we allow our attention and energy to be taken up in efforts to keep others right and remedy their faults, we are wasting precious time. We are like plowmen each of whom has his team to manage and his plow to direct, and in order to keep his furrow straight he must keep his eye on his goal and concentrate on his own task. If he looks to this side and that to see how Tom and Harry are getting on and to

criticize their plowing, then his own furrow will assuredly become crooked.
>> On behalf of Shoghi Effendi, *Living the Life*, p. 10

102. . . . Bahá'u'lláh . . . recognizes that human beings are fallible. He knows that, in our weakness, we shall repeatedly stumble when we try to walk in the path He has pointed out to us. If all human beings became perfect the moment they accepted the call of Bahá'u'lláh this world would be another world. It is in light of our frailty that 'Abdu'l-Bahá appealed to the friends everywhere to love each other and stressed the emphatic teaching of Bahá'u'lláh that each of us should concentrate upon improving his or her own life and ignore the faults of others. How many times the Master stressed the need for unity, for without it His Father's Cause could not go forward.

You have been blessed by recognizing Bahá'u'lláh as the Manifestation of God: your responsibility therefore is to God, irrespective of the actions of your fellow-believers. If every devoted believer withdrew from the Cause as soon as he found the sins of his fellow-Bahá'ís unbearable, who would be left to serve Bahá'u'lláh? All are struggling, with greater or less success to express in their lives the signs and standards that God has laid before them.
>> The Universal House of Justice,
>> to an individual believer, 7/24/73

103. Differences may be creative if they are brought forward in the spirit of Bahá'í unity, or they can be destructive when the motives and spirit are self-centered.
>> The Universal House of Justice,
>> to an individual believer, 8/14/72

104. We note your comment about the lack of love amongst the United States Bahá'ís, and particularly in your community. The best remedy for such an illness is for each believer to be actively and joyfully involved in teaching the Cause, for this activity when undertaken for the love of God promotes

love for one's fellow human beings. No doubt your continued efforts in teaching your contacts will provide a good example for the other friends in your community.
> The Universal House of Justice,
> to an individual believer, 7/23/71

105. The Universal House of Justice has received your letter ... regarding the atmosphere in the United States and your suggestion that it may be timely for the House of Justice to write a letter that would address the "pain of racism" and the consequent "hopelessness and despair" which its persistence occasions. We are to provide the following comments.

The intense focus which you personally have brought to bear on the challenge of dealing with the vital issue of racism in the United States is highly commendable. Action is what is needed. The House of Justice is confident that, as the friends arise, guided by the Writings and the instructions of the beloved Guardian, this enduring, seemingly intractable problem will be ameliorated. It is not certain, however, whether yet another letter will produce the effect you desire. The friends already have in hand copious quotations on the subject from the Central Figures of our Faith together with the interpretations and exhortations of Shoghi Effendi and the further elucidations and calls to action issued by the House of Justice. These have been compiled, as you are perhaps aware, in a volume of some length published by the National Assembly of the United States, in 1986, under the title *The Power of Unity*. And that Assembly has also itself provided a comprehensive statement on the matter, *The Vision of Race Unity*.

The solution to so deep-seated a problem will obviously depend, in large part, on a massive expansion in the number of believers to enable the Bahá'í community to exert the practical influence necessary to bring about profound social change. At the level of the individual, there is no substitute for personal example and for daily renewal of one's spirit through immersion in the Holy Writings and prayer. Studying the life of the Hand of the Cause Louis Gregory also provides a useful and inspiring perspective.

Be assured of the ardent prayers of the House of Justice in the Holy Shrines that your devoted services to the Cause may attract abundant confirmations and that you may be divinely sustained and assisted.

On behalf of The Universal House of Justice,
to an individual believer, 1/20/94

106. The Universal House of Justice received your letter . . . regarding class prejudice in the Bahá'í community, and it has asked us to comment as follows. . . .

The problems related to class prejudice which you have experienced and observed are noted, and the suggestions you offer for working toward their remedy are truly appreciated. As you know, the Bahá'ís are distinguished not by their perfection or their immunity from the negative influences of the wider society in which they live, but by their acceptance of Bahá'u'lláh's vision and willingness to work toward it. Each of us must strike a balance between realistically facing our community's shortcomings, and focusing on Bahá'u'lláh's Teachings rather than our fellow believers as our standard of faith. This comment is not intended to belittle your concerns, but rather to place them in perspective so that you may not become discouraged as you strive toward the ideal.

You are encouraged to share your thoughtful suggestions for raising awareness of this issue with your Local Spiritual Assembly, your National Spiritual Assembly and fellow individual believers. The first step in eradicating any prejudice is education at the local level about the existence of the problem rather than legislation of a particular policy from afar. As you suggest, the Nineteen Day Feast is a perfect forum for beginning consultation on such matters, and further opportunities for education through larger gatherings can always be suggested to the institutions. . . .

Be assured that the Universal House of Justice will pray in the Holy Shrines that your endeavors to serve the Cause of God may be divinely guided and assisted by the Blessed Beauty.

> On behalf of The Universal House of Justice,
> to an individual believer, 5/31/92

107. The Universal House of Justice has received your letter ... conveying your concern about the expression of racial and other prejudices prevailing among Bahá'ís, and indicating your impatience at the slowness of the believers to begin to manifest to a greater degree, both in their individual and community lives, the attributes described in our Teachings governing interpersonal relationships. The House of Justice points out that one of the goals of the Five Year Plan given to every National Spiritual Assembly is to develop "the distinctive character of Bahá'í life, particularly in the local communities." It is important, therefore, that in addition to the tasks of expansion and consolidation, the friends should consciously be working towards a more closely knit loving association. The attainment of this objective, calling as it does for the regeneration by the individual of his character, must be a continuing effort, and your own loving endeavors, along with those of your fellow believers, are essential.

> On behalf of The Universal House of Justice,
> to an individual believer, 3/5/79

108. The Universal House of Justice deeply sympathizes with your frustration at the various incidents described in your letter. . . . We have been instructed to provide the following reply.

That a lack of consciousness and sensitivity to the race issue should manifest itself among certain segments of the

Bahá'í community is troubling, but, given the scope and duration of the problem, is not altogether surprising. The community of the Most Great Name has the divine instructions and the crystal example of 'Abdu'l-Bahá to enable it to make its way from the wilderness of disunity, suspicion and estrangement into the bright sunlight of authentic fellowship, but the journey of transformation is steep and long.

The Central Figures of our Faith, in countless Tablets, illuminate the theme of unity, and by advice and admonition sketch the path toward its achievement. 'Abdu'l-Bahá made it the centerpiece of His public talks during His transcontinental American journey in 1912, even addressing an early meeting of the National Association for the Advancement of Colored People. Shoghi Effendi, writing to the American Bahá'í community in 1938 gave a trenchant analysis of racism and of the means through which it may be effectively resolved (see *The Advent of Divine Justice* 1984 edition, pages 33–41); it is an analysis which should be carefully studied, even memorized, by anyone seriously concerned with this subject. And, in its turn, the House of Justice has repeatedly drawn the attention of the friends to the importance of what the Guardian has termed the "most vital and challenging issue" in various communications, including its Riðván Messages and in the *Promise of World Peace*. Finally, your National Assembly has recently directed a national race unity campaign to focus attention and resources on this issue, and it has been working to stimulate the community to renewed engagement with this deeply rooted problem.

However, there are practical limits to what can be accomplished through appeals and exhortations. Ultimately, any real progress depends upon the sustained, audacious and sincere efforts of the rank and file of believers, guided and motivated by the Sacred Writings and the letters of Shoghi Effendi, working in harmony with their Local Spiritual Assemblies, using Bahá'í consultation, to bring about a change in attitude and behavior. Clearly, all elements of the community must eventually be drawn into this activity. The problem did not appear overnight, however, and the process of healing centuries-old wounds will take time, tremendous perseverance and effort.

It is recommended that you read the biography of the Hand of the Cause Louis Gregory, *To Move the World*, for the insights and inspiration which his courageous example affords. The House of Justice is confident that if you will turn your heart to Bahá'u'lláh, study the Teachings, and undertake to sincerely apply the remedy outlined therein, that you can yourself make a worthy contribution to the amelioration of this scourge which has so long beset the American people.

Regarding Gospel music, the enthusiastic reception accorded the Gospel Choir which performed at the World Congress is evidence that the Bahá'í community is opening itself to music which can richly enhance the quality and spiritual atmosphere of its devotional activities.

As you arise in the path of service, to lend your share to the eradication of this long-standing evil, be assured of the ardent, loving prayers of the House of Justice in the Holy Shrines on your behalf.

> On behalf of The Universal House of Justice,
> to an individual believer, 3/7/93

VI. Justice—in Principle and Application

> *... justice and impartiality... means, in brief,*
> *to regard humanity as a single individual,*
> *and one's own self as a member of that corporeal form,*
> *and to know of a certainty that if*
> *pain or injury afflicts any member of that body,*
> *it must inevitably result in suffering for all the rest.*
> 'Abdu'l-Bahá

109. Assuredly we are today living in the Days of God. These are the glorious days on the like of which the sun hath never risen in the past. These are the days which the people in bygone times eagerly expected. What hath then befallen you that ye are fast asleep? These are the days wherein God hath caused the Day-Star of Truth to shine resplendent. What hath then caused you to keep your silence? These are the appointed days which ye have been yearningly awaiting in the past—the days of the advent of divine justice. Render ye thanks unto God, O ye concourse of believers.
    The Báb, *Selections from the Writings of the Báb*, p. 161

110. The Great Being saith: O well-beloved ones! The tabernacle of unity hath been raised; regard ye not one another as strangers. Ye are the fruits of one tree, and the leaves of one branch. We cherish the hope that the light of justice may shine upon the world and sanctify it from tyranny. If the rulers and kings of the earth, the symbols of the power of God, exalted be His glory, arise and resolve to dedicate themselves to whatever will promote the highest interests of the whole of humanity, the reign of justice will assuredly be established amongst the children of men, and the effulgence of its light will envelop the whole earth. The Great Being saith: The structure of world stability and order hath been reared upon, and will continue to be sustained by, the twin pillars of reward and punishment.... There can be no doubt whatever that if the day star of justice, which the clouds of tyranny have obscured, were to shed its light upon men, the face of the earth would be completely transformed.
    Bahá'u'lláh, *Gleanings*, pp. 218–19

111. Know verily that the essence of justice and the source thereof are both embodied in the ordinances prescribed by Him who is the Manifestation of the Self of God amongst men, if ye be of them that recognize this truth. He doth verily

incarnate the highest, the infallible standard of justice unto all creation. Were His law to be such as to strike terror into the hearts of all that are in heaven and on earth, that law is naught but manifest justice. The fears and agitation which the revelation of this law provokes in men's hearts should indeed be likened to the cries of the suckling babe weaned from his mother's milk, if ye be of them that perceive. Were men to discover the motivating purpose of Gods Revelation, they would assuredly cast away their fears, and, with hearts filled with gratitude, rejoice with exceeding gladness.
    Bahá'u'lláh, *Gleanings,* p. 175

112. "Know thou, of a truth," He significantly affirms, "these great oppressions that have befallen the world are preparing it for the advent of the Most Great Justice." "Say," He again asserts, "he hath appeared with that Justice wherewith mankind hath been adorned, and yet the people are, for the most part, asleep." "The light of men is Justice," He moreover states, "Quench it not with the contrary winds of oppression and tyranny. The purpose of justice is the appearance of unity among men." "No radiance," He declares, "can compare with that of justice. The organization of the world and the tranquillity of mankind depend upon it." "O people of God!" He exclaims, "That which traineth the world is Justice, for it is upheld by two pillars, reward and punishment. These two pillars are the sources of life to the world." "Justice and equity," is yet another assertion, "are two guardians for the protection of man. They have appeared arrayed in their mighty and sacred names to maintain the world in uprightness and protect the nations." "Bestir yourselves, O people," is His emphatic warning, "in anticipation of the days of Divine justice, for the promised hour is now come. Beware lest ye fail to apprehend its import, and be accounted among the erring." "The day is approaching," He similarly has

written, "when the faithful will behold the day-star of justice shining in its full splendor from the day-spring of glory."
> Shoghi Effendi, quoting Bahá'u'lláh in *The Advent of Divine Justice*, p. 23

113. "The whole earth," Bahá'u'lláh, on the other hand, forecasting the bright future in store for a world now wrapt in darkness, emphatically asserts, "is now in a state of pregnancy. The day is approaching when it will have yielded its noblest fruits, when from it will have sprung forth the loftiest trees, the most enchanting blossoms, the most heavenly blessings." "The time is approaching when every created thing will have cast its burden. Glorified be God Who hath vouchsafed this grace that encompasseth all things, whether seen or unseen!" "These great oppressions," He, moreover, foreshadowing humanity's golden age, has written, "are preparing it for the advent of the Most Great Justice." This Most Great Justice is indeed the Justice upon which the structure of the Most Great Peace can alone, and must eventually, rest, while the Most Great Peace will, in turn, usher in that Most Great, that World Civilization which shall remain forever associated with Him Who beareth the Most Great Name.
> Shoghi Effendi, quoting Bahá'u'lláh in *The Promised Day Is Come*, pp. 3–4

114. The amelioration of the conditions of the world reqires the reconstruction of human society and efforts to improve the material well-being of humanity. The Bahá'í approach to this task is evolutionary and multifaceted, involving not only the spiritual transformation of individuals but the establishment of an administrative system based on the application of justice, a system which is at once the "nucleus" and the "pattern" of the future World Order, together with the implementation of programs of social and economic development

that derive their impetus from the grass roots of the community. Such an integrated approach will inevitably create a new world, a world where human dignity is restored and the burden of inequity is lifted from the shoulders of humanity. Then will the generations look back with hertfelt appreciation, for the sacrifices made by Bahá'ís and non-Bahá'ís alike, during this most turbulent period in human history.
 Messages from the Universal House of Justice 1963–1986, no. 425.8

115. O son of man! If thine eyes be turned towards mercy, forsake the things that profit thee, and cleave unto that which will profit mankind. And if thine eyes be turned towards justice, choose thou for thy neighbor that which thou choosest for thyself. Humility exalteth man to the heaven of glory and power, whilst pride abaseth him to the depths of wretchedness and degradation.
 Bahá'u'lláh, *Epistle to the Son of the Wolf*, pp. 29–30

116. Lay not on any soul a load which ye would not wish to be laid upon you, and desire not for any one the things ye would not desire for yourselves. This is My best counsel unto you, did ye but observe it.
 Bahá'u'lláh, *Gleanings*, p. 128

117. O Son of Spirit! The best beloved of all things in My sight is Justice; turn not away therefrom if thou desirest Me, and neglect it not that I may confide in thee. By its aid thou shalt see with thine own eyes and not through the eyes of others, and shalt know of thine own knowledge and not through the knowledge of thy neighbor. Ponder this in thy heart; how it behooveth thee to be. Verily justice is My gift to thee and the sign of My loving-kindness. Set it then before thine eyes.
 Bahá'u'lláh, *The Hidden Words*, Arabic no. 2

118. I testify, O my God, that Thou hast, from eternity, sent down upon Thy servants naught else except that which can

cause them to soar up and be drawn near unto Thee, and to ascend into the heaven of Thy transcendent oneness. Thou hast established Thy bounds among them, and ordained them to stand among Thy creatures as evidences of Thy justice and as signs of Thy mercy, and to be the stronghold of Thy protection amongst Thy people, that no man may in Thy realm transgress against his neighbor.
    Bahá'u'lláh, *Prayers and Meditations*, p. 298

119. It is forbidden you to trade in slaves, be they men or women. It is not for him who is himself a servant to buy another of God's servants, and this hath been prohibited in His Holy Tablets. Thus, by His mercy, hath the commandment been recorded by the Pen of justice. Let no man exalt himself above another; all are but bondslaves before the Lord, and all exemplify the truth that there is none other God but Him. He, verily, is the All-Wise, Whose wisdom encompasseth all things.
    Bahá'u'lláh, *The Kitáb-i-Aqdas*, p. 45

120. [An] attribute of perfection is justice and impartiality. This means to have no regard for one's own personal benefits and selfish advantages, and to carry out the laws of God without the slightest concern for anything else. It means to see one's self as only one of the servants of God, the All-Possessing, and except for aspiring to spiritual distinction, never attempting to be singled out from the others. It means to consider the welfare of the community as one's own. It means, in brief, to regard humanity as a single individual, and one's own self as a member of that corporeal form, and to know of a certainty that if pain or injury afflicts any member of that body, it must inevitably result in suffering for all the rest.
    'Abdu'l Bahá, *The Secret of Divine Civilization*, p. 39

121. At a time when warfare and strife prevailed among nations, when enmity and hatred separated sects and de-

nominations and human differences were very great, Bahá'u'lláh appeared upon the horizon of the East, proclaiming the oneness of God and the unity of the world of humanity. He promulgated the teaching that all mankind are the servants of one God; that all have come into being through the bestowal of the one Creator; that God is kind to all, nurtures, rears and protects all, provides for all and extends His love and mercy to all races and people. Inasmuch as God is loving, why should we be unjust and unkind? As God manifests loyalty and mercy, why should we show forth enmity and hatred? Surely the divine policy is more perfect than human plan and theory; for no matter how wise and sagacious man may become, he can never attain a policy that is superior to the policy of God. Therefore, we must emulate the attitude of God, love all people, be just and kind to every human creature.

'Abdu'l-Bahá, *The Promulgation of Universal Peace*, p. 174

122. The man who thinks only of himself and is thoughtless of others is undoubtedly inferior to the animal because the animal is not possessed of the reasoning faculty. The animal is excused; but in man there is reason, the faculty of justice, the faculty of mercifulness. Possessing all these faculties he must not leave them unused. He who is so hard-hearted as to think only of his own comfort, such an one will not be called man.

'Abdu'l-Bahá, *Foundations of World Unity*, p. 42

123. A financier with colossal wealth should not exist whilst near him is a poor man in dire necessity. When we see poverty allowed to reach a condition of starvation it is a sure sign that somewhere we shall find tyranny. Men must bestir themselves in this matter, and no longer delay in altering conditions which bring the misery of grinding poverty to a very large number of the people. The rich must give of their abundance, they must soften their hearts and cultivate a compassionate intelligence, taking thought for those sad

ones who are suffering from lack of the very necessities of life.

There must be special laws made, dealing with these extremes of riches and of want. The members of the Government should consider the laws of God when they are framing plans for the ruling of the people. The general rights of mankind must be guarded and preserved.

The government of the countries should conform to the Divine Law which gives equal justice to all. This is the only way in which the deplorable superfluity of great wealth and miserable, demoralizing, degrading poverty can be abolished. Not until this is done will the Law of God be obeyed.
'Abdu'l-Bahá, *Paris Talks*, pp. 153–54

124. Bahá'u'lláh teaches that an equal standard of human rights must be recognized and adopted. In the estimation of God all men are equal; there is no distinction or preferment for any soul in the dominion of His justice and equity.
'Abdu'l-Bahá, *Bahá'í World Faith*, pp. 240–41

125. Oh, friends of God, be living examples of justice! So that by the Mercy of God, the world may see in your actions that you manifest the attributes of justice and mercy.

Justice is not limited, it is a universal quality. Its operation must be carried out in all classes, from the highest to the lowest. Justice must be sacred, and the rights of all the people must be considered. Desire for others only that which you desire for yourselves. Then shall we rejoice in the Sun of Justice, which shines from the Horizon of God.

Each man has been placed in a post of honor, which he must not desert. A humble workman who commits an injustice is as much to blame as a renowned tyrant. Thus we all have our choice between justice and injustice.

I hope that each one of you will become just, and direct your thoughts towards the unity of mankind; that you will never harm your neighbors nor speak ill of any one; that you

will respect the rights of all men, and be more concerned for the interests of others than for your own. Thus will you become torches of Divine justice, acting in accordance with the Teaching of Bahá'u'lláh, who, during His life, bore innumerable trials and persecutions in order to show forth to the world of mankind the virtues of the World of Divinity, making it possible for you to realize the supremacy of the spirit, and to rejoice in the Justice of God.
'Abdu'l-Bahá, *Paris Talks*, pp. 159–60

126. "God be praised!" 'Abdu'l-Bahá, in His turn, exclaims, "The sun of justice hath risen above the horizon of Bahá'u'lláh. For in His Tablets the foundations of such a justice have been laid as no mind hath, from the beginning of creation, conceived." "The canopy of existence," He further explains, "resteth upon the pole of justice, and not of forgiveness, and the life of mankind dependeth on justice and not on forgiveness."

Small wonder, therefore, that the Author of the Bahá'í Revelation should have chosen to associate the name and title of that House, which is to be the crowning glory of His administrative institutions, not with forgiveness but with justice, to have made justice the only basis and the permanent foundation of His Most Great Peace, and to have proclaimed it in His Hidden Words as "the best beloved of all things" in His sight. It is to the American believers, particularly, that I feel urged to direct this fervent plea to ponder in their hearts the implications of this moral rectitude, and to uphold, with heart and soul and uncompromisingly, both individually and collectively, this sublime standard–a standard of which justice is so essential and potent an element.
Shoghi Effendi, *The Advent of Divine Justice*, pp. 28–29

127. As regards the passages in the sacred writings indicating the wrath of God; Shoghi Effendi says that the Divinity has

many attributes: He is loving and merciful but also just. Just as reward and punishment, according to Bahá'u'lláh, are the pillars upon which society rests, so mercy and justice may be considered as their counterpart in the world to come. Should we disobey God and work against His commands He will view our acts in the light of justice and punish us for it. That punishment may not be in the form of fire, as some believe, but in the form of spiritual deprivation and degradation. This is why we read so often in the prayers statements such as "God do not deal with us with justice, but rather through thy infinite mercy." The wrath of God is in the administration of His justice, both in this world and in the world to come. A God that is only loving or only just is not a perfect God. The divinity has to possess both of these aspects as every father ought to express both in his attitude towards his children. If we ponder a while, we will see that our welfare can be insured only when both of these divine attributes are equally emphasized and practiced.
>   On behalf of Shoghi Effendi, *Arohanui: Letters to New Zealand*, pp. 32–33

128. To discriminate against any race, on the ground of its being socially backward, politically immature, and numerically in a minority, is a flagrant violation of the spirit that animates the Faith of Bahá'u'lláh. The consciousness of any division or cleavage in its ranks is alien to its very purpose, principles, and ideals. Once its members have fully recognized the claim of its Author, and, by identifying themselves with its Administrative Order, accepted unreservedly the principles and laws embodied in its teachings, every differentiation of class, creed, or color must automatically be obliterated, and never be allowed, under any pretext, and however great the pressure of events or of public opinion, to reassert itself. If any discrimination is at all to be tolerated, it should be a discrimination not against, but rather in favor of

the minority, be it racial or otherwise. Unlike the nations and peoples of the earth, be they of the East or of the West, democratic or authoritarian, communist or capitalist, whether belonging to the Old World or the New, who either ignore, trample upon, or extirpate, the racial, religious, or political minorities within the sphere of their jurisdiction, every organized community enlisted under the banner of Bahá'u'lláh should feel it to be its first and inescapable obligation to nurture, encourage, and safeguard every minority belonging to any faith, race, class, or nation within it. So great and vital is this principle that in such circumstances, as when an equal number of ballots have been cast in an election, or where the qualifications for any office are balanced as between the various races, faiths or nationalities within the community, priority should unhesitatingly be accorded the party representing the minority, and this for no other reason except to stimulate and encourage it, and afford it an opportunity to further the interests of the community. In the light of this principle, and bearing in mind the extreme desirability of having the minority elements participate and share responsibility in the conduct of Bahá'í activity, it should be the duty of every Bahá'í community so to arrange its affairs that in cases where individuals belonging to the divers minority elements within it are already qualified and fulfill the necessary requirements, Bahá'í representative institutions, be they Assemblies, conventions, conferences, or committees, may have represented on them as many of these divers elements, racial or otherwise, as possible. The adoption of such a course, and faithful adherence to it, would not only be a source of inspiration and encouragement to those elements that are numerically small and inadequately represented, but would demonstrate to the world at large the universality and representative character of the Faith of Bahá'u'lláh, and the freedom of His followers from the taint of those preju-

dices which have already wrought such havoc in the domestic affairs, as well as the foreign relationships, of the nations.
Shoghi Effendi, *The Advent of Divine Justice*, pp. 29–30

129. What is not clearly defined is "majority" and "minority." The Guardian refers to "various races, faiths or nationalities." Where this is obvious, e.g. in the United States a white American and a Negro, there is no problem. In all cases of doubt a re-vote should be held.
The Universal House of Justice, *Lights of Guidance*, p. 15

130. In this connection, however, he wishes me to stress the fact that the two races should ultimately be brought together, and be urged to associate with the utmost unity and fellowship, and be given full and equal opportunity to participate in the conduct of the teachings as well as administrative activities of the Faith. Nothing short of such ultimate fusion of the two races can ensure the faithful application of that cornerstone principle of the Cause regarding the oneness of mankind.
On behalf of Shoghi Effendi, *Bahá'í News*, no. 108, 6/37, pp. 1–2

131. The friends should bear in mind that in our Faith, unlike every other society, the minority, to compensate for what might be treated as an inferior status, receives special attention, love and consideration. . . .
On behalf of Shoghi Effendi, *A Special Measure of Love*, p. 20

132. On principle no discrimination whatsoever should be made between the white and the colored believers in any administrative function or duty. The Cause stands above any racial consideration, for the core of its message is the principle of the oneness of mankind. The colored believers are entitled to the very same privileges and opportunities of service which their fellow-believers of the white race enjoy.

This principle is quite clear, and should be always emphasized without any compromise of any kind. Its application, however, to individual cases is the responsibility of the assemblies.
> On behalf of Shoghi Effendi, *The Power of Unity*, p. 80

133. . . . it is of the greatest importance that the Bahá'ís and more especially the youth—should demonstrate actively our complete lack of prejudice and indeed, our prejudices in favor of minorities. . . .
> Shoghi Effendi, *Lights of Guidance*, p. 511

134. As followers of God's Holy Faith it is our obligation to protect the just interests of any minority element within the Bahá'í community. In fact in the administration of our Bahá'í affairs, representatives of minority groups are not only enabled to enjoy equal rights and privileges, but they are even favored and accorded priority. Bahá'ís should be careful never to deviate from this noble standard, even if the course of events or public opinion should bring pressure to bear upon them.

The principles in the Writings are clear, but usually it is when these principles are applied that questions arise. In all cases where the correct course of action is not clear believers should consult their National Spiritual Assembly who will exercise their judgment in advising the friends on the best course to follow.
> The Universal House of Justice, *Messages from the Universal House of Justice*, pp. 49–50

Six

African Americans and Teaching the Faith of Bahá'u'lláh

I. Offering the Message of Bahá'u'lláh to People of African Ancestry

> *The Guardian will pray*
> *that you will be confirmed in your efforts*
> *to teach more Negroes.*
> *They have been subject so long*
> *to the prejudices of the majority peoples,*
> *that he hopes they will find*
> *their goal in the Cause of God.*
> Shoghi Effendi

1. Regarding the teaching work among the colored; the Guardian wishes to assure Mr. . . . that the universality of the Faith of Bahá'u'lláh imperatively requires the believers to teach it to all peoples, irrespective of their race, class or origin. The Message of this day is directed to the whole of mankind, not to any particular section of it. The colored as well as the noncolored are both welcomed into the Bahá'í Community, and once they enter its ranks they are recognized as one and the same. Rather they should cease to look at the racial differences separating them, and should associate with each other in perfect peace, unity and fellowship.

The Bahá'ís should by all means endeavor to attract to the Faith as many members of the colored race as they possibly can, and thus demonstrate in deeds the universality of the Message of Bahá'u'lláh. It is only through this intermingling of races within the framework of His World Order that a lasting and just solution can be found to the perplexing racial issues confronting mankind.
On behalf of Shoghi Effendi, to an individual believer, 11/19/37

2. His prayers for the success of your activities, particularly in connection with interracial amity work, are being continually offered at the Threshold of Bahá'u'lláh, that through His guidance you may effectively assist in spreading the Message among the colored people, and thus vindicate the universality of the Faith.
On behalf of Shoghi Effendi, 1/26/37

3. He was very pleased to hear you have a Community of eleven believers there and that you have recently welcomed into the Faith the first Negro believer of that city. No doubt her presence will strengthen you all in your services to the Cause, as you are now able to exemplify in your own group the principles for which we stand.
On behalf of Shoghi Effendi, to a local Assembly, 1/16/45

4. We cannot very well prosecute a teaching campaign successfully...if we do not in our home communities demonstrate to the fullest extent our love for the people who spring from the African population!
On behalf of Shoghi Effendi, *Bahá'í Youth*, p. 18

5. Indeed if the friends could seek, and exert themselves, to become 100 per cent Bahá'ís they would see how greatly their influence over others would be increased, and how rapidly the Cause would spread. The world is seeking not a compromise but the embodiment of a high and shining ideal. The

more the friends live up to our teachings in every aspect of their lives, in their homes, in business, in their social relationships, the greater will be the attraction they exercise over the hearts of others.

He is pleased to see you have naturally, with conviction and good will towards all, been mingling with and teaching the colored people. When the Bahá'ís live up to their teachings as they should, although it may arouse the opposition of some it will arouse still more the admiration of fair minded people.

On behalf of Shoghi Effendi, *The Bahá'í Life*, p. 11

6. He feels that as the main object of the Bahá'í interracial work is to abolish prejudice against any and every race and minority group, it is obviously proper for them to include in particular any group that is receiving especially bad treatment—such as the Japanese-Americans are being subjected to. There is also no reason why work should not be done among and in cooperation with the Mexicans, the Chinese and so on.

He has always been very anxious to have the Indians taught and enlisted under the banner of the Faith, in view of the Master's remarkable statements about the possibilities of their future and that they represent the aboriginal American population.

The Negroes, likewise, are, one might say, a key problem and epitomize the feelings of color prejudice so rife in the United States. That is why he has so constantly emphasized the importance of the Bahá'ís actively and continuously demonstrating that in the Faith this cruel and horrible taint of discrimination against, and contempt for, them does not exist but on the contrary is supplanted by a feeling of esteem for their great gifts and a complete lack of prejudice in every field of life.

On behalf of Shoghi Effendi, *Bahá'í News*, no. 188, 10/46, pp. 3–4

7. At a time when the United States government is making every effort to eliminate racial discrimination, the Bahá'ís cannot be too careful to point out that they have, ever since the inception of the Faith in America, been upholding its fundamental teaching in this respect, and been seeking to enlist in its ranks the truth-seekers amongst the Negroes. It would be a great pity, indeed, if the Negro race should ever come to feel that our true friendship was offered them only when the prejudice against them began to wane throughout the country, and not in their greatest days of suffering and need.
On behalf of Shoghi Effendi, to an individual believer, 10/16/42

8. It is only natural that people should be able to pour out more freely their enthusiasm in the field of services that lies nearest to their heart, and if your departure would in no way affect the assembly status . . . he sees no reason why you should not go and teach among the Negroes, as this is a very important field of Bahá'í activity, especially so in these days when the racial question seems to be coming to a head in the United States. The more Negroes who become Bahá'ís, the greater the leaven will be within their own race, working for harmony and friendship between these two bodies of American citizens: the white and the colored.
On behalf of Shoghi Effendi, *The Power of Unity*, p. 107

9. He was also very pleased to hear about the new Negro element in the Cause, and he hopes that the Bahá'í Assemblies and Committees will utilize this new talent to the full. Perhaps great suffering for America could be averted if the Cause were not only more widely and quickly spread but the solidarity of races within its ranks more conspicuously demonstrated. He deeply appreciates your services in this important field of Bahá'í activity—racial unity.
On behalf of Shoghi Effendi, *The Power of Unity*, p. 78

10. The Guardian was happy to see that so many of those in attendance were Negroes—and that the subject of discussion was eliminating race prejudice and attracting more Negroes. The real means of eliminating race prejudice, is to spread and establish the Faith; for in it, there is no prejudice whatsoever, as the Faith itself holds as its cardinal principle, the Oneness of Humanity.

The Guardian will pray that you will be confirmed in your efforts to teach more Negroes. They have been subject so long to the prejudices of the majority peoples, that he hopes they will find their goal in the Cause of God. In Africa the Faith is spreading very rapidly among the Negroes, and there are now more Negroes in the Faith in Africa, where the Faith has been established less than four years, than there are in America, where the Faith has existed for 60 years. The Friends should concentrate on pure hearted people, and continue association and fellowship with them, until they themselves become active workers in the Cause of God.

> On behalf of Shoghi Effendi, to an individual believer, 12/20/55

11. You should... concentrate your efforts on teaching all you can, particularly endeavoring to attract and confirm in the Faith the Negroes, as the number of Negro Bahá'ís in the United States should be many times larger than it is at present.

> On behalf of Shoghi Effendi, to an individual believer, 9/19/57

12. Let anyone who feels the urge among the participators in this crusade, which embraces all the races, all the republics, classes and denominations of the entire Western Hemisphere, arise, and, circumstances permitting, direct in particular the attention, and win eventually the unqualified adherence, of the Negro, the Indian, the Eskimo, and Jewish races to his Faith. No more laudable and meritorious service can be rendered the Cause of God, at the present hour, than

a successful effort to enhance the diversity of the members of the American Bahá'í community by swelling the ranks of the Faith through the enrollment of the members of these races. A blending of these highly differentiated elements of the human race, harmoniously interwoven into the fabric of an all-embracing Bahá'í fraternity, and assimilated through the dynamic processes of a divinely-appointed Administrative Order, and contributing each its share to the enrichment and glory of Bahá'í community life, is surely an achievement the contemplation of which must warm and thrill every Bahá'í heart.

    Shoghi Effendi, *The Advent of Divine Justice*, p. 45

13. The Americas have been a melting pot and a meeting place for the races of men, and the need is acute for the fulfillment of God's promises of the realization of the oneness of mankind. Particularly do the Master and the Guardian point to the Afro-Americans and the Amerindians, two great ethnic groups whose spiritual powers will be released through their response to the Creative Word. But our Teachings must touch all, must include all peoples. And, in this hour of your tireless activity, what special rewards shall come to those who will arise, summoned by 'Abdu'l-Bahá's Words: "Now is the time to divest yourselves of the garment of attachment to this phenomenal realm, be wholly severed from the physical world, become angels of heaven, and travel and teach through all these regions."

    The Universal House of Justice, *Messages from the Universal House of Justice*, pp. 73–74

II. The Need for Perseverance, Courage and Wisdom

> *The friends must remember*
> *that the cardinal principle of their Faith*
> *is the Oneness of Mankind.*
> *This places an obligation on them*
> *far surpassing the obligation*
> *which Christian charity and brotherly love*
> *places upon the Christians.*
> *They should demonstrate this spirit of oneness*
> *constantly and courageously. . . .*
> Shoghi Effendi

14. As to the racial aspects of your work Shoghi Effendi believes that no chances should be lost, for the Master stressed constantly the importance of reconciling the Negro and white people of North America. This field of service not only attracts the attention of innumerable persons to the Cause, but also furthers one of the ideals of the Faith, namely the abolition of racial prejudice.
On behalf of Shoghi Effendi, *The Power of Unity*, pp. 106–07

15. I wish you to persevere despite seemingly insurmountable obstacles and to rest assured that my prayers will continue to be offered in your behalf. Concentrate on your work for the colored, for this is a work that will attract the mightiest confirmations and blessings of Bahá'u'lláh and will earn you the abiding gratitude of future generations in the Cause.
Shoghi Effendi, *Bahá'í News*, no. 58, 1/32, p. 1

16. The holding of public meetings in that city should be avoided only in case it would lead to grave and very serious results. Slight local criticisms and unpopularity should not act as a deterrent. The issue should be met squarely and courageously, and an effort should be made to attract at first

the most cultured element among the colored, and through them establish contact with the white and the masses. Such individuals and groups, whether white or colored, who are relatively free from racial prejudice, should be approached, separately if necessary, and an endeavor should be made to bring them together eventually, not only on formal occasions and for specific purposes, but in intimate social gatherings, in private homes as well as in formally recognized Bahá'í centers.
On behalf of Shoghi Effendi, *Bahá'í News*, no. 103, 10/36, p. 1

17. As regards the interracial meetings held in your home; the Guardian wishes you by all means to maintain them, and to invite those white believers who are willing to assist you in this work to participate in these gatherings. But, as always, you should take great care not to openly wound the feelings of the noncolored population. The racial problem, whether in America or elsewhere should, indeed, be tackled with the utmost tact and moderation, but also with conscious, firm and absolute loyalty to the spirit as well as to the actual word of the Bahá'í teaching of the Oneness of Mankind.
On behalf of Shoghi Effendi, 1/26/37

18. In connection with the developments reported in the *Washington Post*—copies of which you were kind enough to send the Guardian—concerning the concert which was given by the famous colored singer Miss Anderson; these events, which clearly show how deep-rooted and intense is racial prejudice in America, should awaken the friends to a deeper realization of the unique responsibility that is theirs, as the founders of the New World Order of Bahá'u'lláh, to combat courageously and relentlessly the false racial doctrines, and inveterate racial hatreds that so sadly poison the hearts and minds of their fellow-countrymen, and of such increasingly growing number of the peoples and nations of the world.

More than ever today it is their vital duty to proclaim, boldly and unequivocally, the essential and underlying unity of all human races, and to demonstrate how the unifying Spirit released in this age through Bahá'u'lláh has succeeded in making this ideal a living and working reality.
      On behalf of Shoghi Effendi, *The Power of Unity*, pp. 84–85

19. The Guardian fully realizes the difficulties in the South of teaching both the colored and white. They both have prejudice, and while the white people are proud and consider themselves to be superior, the Negroes are suspicious and oversensitive through suffering and oppression. He hopes, however, that you will be able to confirm believers of both races.
      On behalf of Shoghi Effendi, to an individual believer, 10/19/41

20. Regarding the whole manner of teaching the Faith in the South: the Guardian feels that, although the greatest consideration should be shown the feelings of white people in the South whom we are teaching, under no circumstances should we discriminate in their favor, consider them more valuable to the Cause than their Negro fellow-southerners, or single them out to be taught the Message first. To pursue such a policy, however necessary and even desirable it may superficially seem, would be to compromise the true spirit of our Faith, which permits us to make no such distinctions in offering its tenets to the world. The Negro and white races should be offered, simultaneously, on a basis of equality, the Message of Bahá'u'lláh. Rich or poor, known or unknown, should be permitted to hear of this Holy Faith in this, humanity's greatest hour of need.

    This does not mean that we should go against the laws of the state, pursue a radical course which will stir up trouble, and cause misunderstanding. On the contrary, the Guardian feels that, where no other course is open, the two races should be taught separately until they are fully conscious of the implications of being a Bahá'í, and then be confirmed and admitted to voting membership. Once, however, this has happened, they cannot shun each other's company, and feel the Cause to be like other Faiths in the South, with separate white and black compartments. . . .

. . . 'Abdu'l-Bahá Himself set the perfect example to the American believers in this matter—as in every other. He was tactful, but the essence of courage, and showed no favoritism to the white people as opposed to their dark-skinned compatriots. No matter how sincere and devoted the white believers in the South may be, there is no reason why they should be the ones to decide when and how the Negro Southerner shall hear of the Cause of God; both must be taught by whoever rises to spread the Message in those parts.
On behalf of Shoghi Effendi, *The Power of Unity*, pp. 82–83

21. These, indeed, are the days when heroism is needed on the part of the believers. Self-sacrifice, courage, indomitable hope and confidence are characteristics they should show forth, because these very attributes cannot but fix the attention of the public and lead them to inquire what, in a world so hopelessly chaotic and bewildered, leads these people to be so assured, so confident, so full of devotion? Increasingly, as time goes by, the characteristics of the Bahá'ís will be that which captures the attention of their fellow-citizens. They must show their aloofness from the hatreds and recriminations which are tearing at the hearts of humanity, and demonstrate by deed and word their profound belief in the future peaceful unification of the entire human race.
Shoghi Effendi, *Bahá'í News*, no. 157, 11/42, p. 1

22. We must always remember that the Cause is universal and that while local inhabitants of a district may live according to a certain code we as Bahá'ís must live up to the Faith.

We cannot compromise on these major issues, or we would find that in almost every part of the globe the believers had abandoned some prime tenent of their Faith to oblige public opinion. This does not mean you cannot teach white people in a separate fireside meeting. But we must be very careful to never give anyone any grounds for saying we are retreating from our cardinal principle—the oneness of mankind. . . .
On behalf of Shoghi Effendi, to an individual believer, 7/30/46

23. The attitude toward teaching the Faith in the southern states of the United States should be entirely changed. For years, in the hope of attracting the white people, in order to "go easy" with them and not offend their sensibilities, a compromise has been made in the teaching work throughout the South. The results have been practically nil. The white people have not responded worth mentioning, to the Faith, and the colored people have been hurt and also have not responded.

He feels it is time that the Bahá'ís stopped worrying entirely about the white element in a community, and that they should concentrate on showing the Negro element that this is a Faith which produces full equality and which loves and wants minorities. The Bahá'ís should welcome the Negroes to their homes, make every effort to teach them, associate with them, even marry them if they want to. We must remember that 'Abdu'l-Bahá Himself united in Bahá'í marriage a colored and a white believer. He could not do more.
On behalf of Shoghi Effendi, in *To Move the World*, p. 294

24. He feels that adequate action has not yet been taken in America to properly fulfill the injunctions of the Master in this very vital matter. The Guardian feels that special effort must be made to teach the Negroes and especially in the South, and this should be done without regard to whatever teaching work may or may not be done of the white people....

If there should be some criticism from the white people the Guardian feels this will not be harmful because they have not responded to the Call in the South and therefore any objection they may raise could have no substantial basis. On the other hand if they learn the Bahá'ís are concentrating on bringing the Message of Unity to the Negroes that may arouse some interest and perhaps stir some special interest on their part.
    On behalf of Shoghi Effendi, *The Power of Unity*, pp. 108-09

25. He also feels that particular attention should be devoted to the teaching work in the South, and to attracting the colored people. The years of careful attention, which have been devoted to the white element in the South, in the hope of placating them, enrolling them in the Faith, and also enrolling the colored Bahá'ís at the same time, have not shown satisfactory results. In view of this, he urges the friends to concentrate on teaching the Negroes. They should be courageous in their racial stand, particularly as so many non-Bahá'ís and non-Bahá'í organizations are showing marked courage at this time, when the decisions of the Supreme Court are being so hotly contested in the South. The friends must remember that the cardinal principle of their Faith is the Oneness of Mankind. This places an obligation on them far surpassing the obligation which Christian charity and brotherly love places upon the Christians. They should demonstrate this spirit of oneness constantly and courageously in the South.
    On behalf of Shoghi Effendi, *Bahá'í News*, no. 321, 11/57, insert

III. African Americans as Teachers of the Faith in America

> *... their contribution to the Cause is much needed,*
> *especially as there is a lack of Negro Bahá'í teachers*
> *who can go out to their own people*
> *along with their white brothers and sisters,*
> *and convince them of the active universality of our Faith.*
> Shoghi Effendi

26. The source of courage and power is the promotion of the Word of God, and steadfastness in His Love.
Bahá'u'lláh, *Tablets of Bahá'u'lláh*, p. 156

27. The Negro believers must be just as active as their white brothers and sisters in spreading the Faith, both among their own race and members of other races.
On behalf of Shoghi Effendi, *Lights of Guidance*, p. 402

28. The qualities of heart so richly possessed by the Negro are much needed in the world today—their great capacity for faith, their loyalty and devotion to their religion when once they believe, their purity of heart, God has richly endowed them, and their contribution to the Cause is much needed, especially as there is a lack of Negro Bahá'í teachers who can go out to their own people along with their white brothers and sisters, and convince them of the active universality of our Faith. He will especially pray that you may confirm souls of capacity in this field.
On behalf of Shoghi Effendi, *Lights of Guidance*, p. 403

29. The colored friends need the Faith very much, as they have suffered and been downtrodden in the past a great deal, and they must realize that in the propagation of the Revelation of Bahá'u'lláh lies their hope for a better future, just as much as the hope of the entire world.
On behalf of Shoghi Effendi, *Lights of Guidance*, p. 411

30. . . . Shoghi Effendi thinks that the place you are needed most is America. The Master asked you to work for the colored and among them and Shoghi Effendi would urge you to do the same. Your own people need you most and you have a duty towards them that you have to fulfill.

. . . You should take up a work that will give you ample time to teach among the colored.
On behalf of Shoghi Effendi, to an individual believer, 10/20/32

31. He [the Guardian] was very happy to know that you are so active in the administrative work of the Cause, and he hopes that you will also find time to teach your people the Faith. Gifted and devoted as you are you should be able to profoundly interest and guide them.
On behalf of Shoghi Effendi, to an individual believer, 11/23/41

32. Before closing I wish to draw your attention to the ardent plea made by the Guardian in his last general letter, *The Advent of Divine Justice,* regarding the extension of the teaching work among the Negroes, and to urge you, as the outstanding Bahá'í teacher in this field, to redouble your efforts in this connection, so that an increasing number of distinguished and capable members of that race may be enlisted under the banner of Bahá'u'lláh, and through their presence in the Community help in further adding to the variety and richness of its membership, and in reinforcing its strength, vitality and influence.
On behalf of Shoghi Effendi, to an individual believer, 4/27/39

33. . . . the Guardian's heart [was] immeasurably gladdened at the report of the outstanding teaching achievements which you and Mr. Gregory have been able to accomplish in Pine Bluff during this past year. His heart goes out in deepest gratitude to you both for all the sacrifice, determination and resourceful energy you have displayed all through your teaching work in that center, and he feels indescribably

happy and encouraged to know that as a result the entire Negro population of Pine Bluff has heard of the Cause, that one of the college students . . . has already declared herself a believer, and that several others are on the point of becoming fully confirmed. . . .

In view of these remarkable results you have accomplished in Pine Bluff, particularly among the student body in the Arkansas State College, and notwithstanding any opposition, veiled or open, which may be directed against you from certain quarters, the Guardian would strongly urge you to remain in that center, and to confidently persist in your efforts until you succeed in establishing a strong and united group of confirmed believers, capable of developing eventually into a local assembly. He wishes you, in particular, to concentrate on teaching the Negro inhabitants of Pine Bluff, and thus bring into the Cause this hitherto neglected, though highly promising and spiritually receptive, element of the population in the Southern States.
On behalf of Shoghi Effendi, in *To Move the World*, pp. 255–56

34. The more Negroes who become Bahá'ís, the greater the leaven will be within their own race, working for harmony and friendship between these two bodies of American citizens: the white and the colored.
On behalf of Shoghi Effendi, *The Power of Unity*, p. 107

35. He feels that you should try to attract some white members to the Cause in your City, for just the same reason that other groups, preponderatingly white in membership, seek to attract Colored members, in order to demonstrate the universality of our Faith. Otherwise, in the sight of God, there is no distinction. . . .

Indeed he is very pleased to see that the Negro friends are so devoted and spiritually minded and that in certain places whole groups and communities of them exist.
On behalf of Shoghi Effendi, to a Bahá'í Group, 11/20/44

IV. Teaching and Serving in the African American Community

> *Fundamental changes in social attitude*
> *will be most readily achieved*
> *if the relevant spiritual and moral principles*
> *are courageously set forth*
> *and if men and women of good will*
> *can see others attempting successfully to give these ideals*
> *practical expression in individual and community life.*
> The Universal House of Justice

36. A man may be a Bahá'í in name only. If he is a Bahá'í in reality, his deeds and actions will be decisive proofs of it. What are the requirements? Love for mankind, sincerity towards all, reflecting the oneness of the world of humanity, philanthropy, becoming enkindled with the fire of the love of God, attainment to the knowledge of God and that which is conducive to human welfare.
'Abdu'l-Bahá, *The Promulgation of Universal Peace*, p. 336

37. Most important of all is that love and unity should prevail in the Bahá'í community, as this is what people are most longing for in the present dark state of the world. Words without the living example will never be sufficient to breathe hope into the hearts of a disillusioned and often cynical generation.
Shoghi Effendi, *Lights of Guidance*, p. 303

38. ... all Bahá'ís can help ... by working more actively ... to break down racial barriers, and to foster loving association with minority groups. The Bahá'ís should go out amongst such groups and include them in their activities as much as possible.
On behalf of Shoghi Effendi, *The Power of Unity*, p. 105

39. The Guardian feels he should urge your Assembly that ... you should always bear in mind that only through strict

and loyal adherence to the Bahá'í principle of racial unity and fellowship can you hope to lay down a firm and enduring basis for the acceptance and entry of the colored races into the Community.
> On behalf of Shoghi Effendi, *The Power of Unity*, p. 108

40. The report of the teaching activities of the two groups greatly pleased Shoghi Effendi, for he has been always emphasizing the importance of the interracial amity work. It is surely wonderful to have such mixed groups of Negro and white friends take the trip to the south and bring the Message of Bahá'u'lláh. This way we will be putting into practice the spirit of amity between the races which we advocate. Shoghi Effendi hopes that this program of work will be pursued and innumerable souls attracted to the Cause.
> On behalf of Shoghi Effendi, to an individual believer, 1/15/32

41. Regarding the problem of teaching in districts of mixed colored and white populations, the Guardian fully approves of the policy adopted by the National Spiritual Assembly to the effect that the teaching work should be carried simultaneously with the two races in the south without the slightest discrimination. For the Teachings are obviously not intended for only one race or one class. Your Assembly's suggestion that Bahá'í public meetings should henceforth be conducted separately for whites and colored and that study classes resulting from such meetings should likewise be conducted separately until individuals of both races are truly confirmed believers is splendid as it will undoubtedly help in removing the misunderstandings and obstacles that have thus far stood in the way of the expansion of the Faith in the Southern States. To alienate either the white or the colored race would be indeed unfair and unjustifiable. The solution proposed by your Assembly thus marks a step in advance over the methods which the friends have hitherto enforced in their teaching work in the Southern States. The Guardian therefore trusts

that it will be brought fully to the attention of the friends, and that they will each and all arise to apply it in their future teaching activities.

In this connection, however, he wishes me to stress the fact that the two races should ultimately be brought together, and be urged to associate with the utmost unity and fellowship, and be given full and equal opportunity to participate in the conduct of the teachings as well as administrative activities of the Faith. Nothing short of such ultimate fusion of the two races can ensure the faithful application of that cornerstone principle of the Cause regarding the oneness of mankind.

On behalf of Shoghi Effendi, *Bahá'í News*, no. 108, 6/37, pp. 1–2

42. In the matter of teaching, as repeatedly and emphatically stated, particularly in his *Advent of Divine Justice*, the Guardian does not wish the believers to make the slightest discrimination, even though this may result in provoking opposition or criticism from any individual, class or institution. The call of Bahá'u'lláh, being universal, should be addressed with equal force to all the peoples, classes and nations of the world, irrespective of any religious, racial, political or class distinctions or differences.

In America, where racial prejudice is still so widely prevalent, it is the responsibility of the believers to combat and uproot it with all their force, first by endeavoring to introduce into the Cause as many . . . minority groups as they can approach and teach, and second by stimulating close fellowship and intercourse between them and the rest of the Community.

On behalf of Shoghi Effendi, to an individual believer, 1/20/41

43. He does not feel it is good to canvas Negro people in their houses or places of business, for this in itself looks like a kind of discrimination. They should be invited to our meetings on

the same footing as other people and reached by the same methods, public or private. If a Negro Bahá'í speaker were going to give a public Bahá'í address then it would be appropriate to send special invitations to a Negro mailing list. But the friends should seek out the colored people and make friends with them and associate with them in the same social ways they do with their white friends. This alone will attract the colored people, not words, but a real, unassuming, demonstration that the Bahá'ís are willing and glad to associate with them, eat with them, and be seen in public with them. . . .
 On behalf of Shoghi Effendi, to an individual believer, 7/7/49

44. He is very pleased to hear the assembly there is active and attracting new souls to the Faith, and he hopes that gradually the colored friends at the College . . . will feel moved to embrace the Cause. Perhaps if some of the young Negro Bahá'í teachers visited with them they would be more convinced that the Cause belongs to no race but to all those who accept it and work for it.
 On behalf of Shoghi Effendi, to an individual believer, 3/12/49

45. He attaches great importance to the contact work in the States with African students. This is a field many friends can take part in at home.
 On behalf of Shoghi Effendi, to the Africa Committee, 9/7/51,

46. He hopes that wherever it is possible the believers will make every effort to contact African students and visitors, and to show them kindness and hospitality. This may not only lead to the conversion of some while in America, but will also make friends for the Faith in Africa.
 On behalf of Shoghi Effendi, to the friends at Louhelen, 9/28/51

47. Your Committee . . . . should also, as part of its work, urge the Bahá'ís, wherever they may be, to devote more attention

to the minorities. This is particularly true in places where there are universities where foreign students belonging to the black, yellow and brown races are studying. In this way, the friends cannot only obey one of the most beautiful principles of our Faith, to show hospitality to the stranger in our midst, but also demonstrate the universality of our Teachings, and the true brotherhood that animates us, and in addition, confirm Bahá'ís who may go back to the distant places of the earth—the Pacific, Africa, Asia, etc., and be of inestimable help to the newly-born Bahá'í Communities.

Likewise the friends should carry their friendship and their teachings to other minority groups in America, such as the Italians, the Jews, the Czechs, the Poles, the Russians, etc.

He hopes your Committee will constantly bear in mind these points, and that you will try to meet with as many people personally as possible. Teaching trips, lectures, example, have more effect than the circular of printed matter, which half the time is not properly read and assimilated.
> On behalf of Shoghi Effendi to the Bahá'í Inter-Racial Teaching Committee, 5/27/57

48. The summer schools provide a splendid setting and environment to which the best element among the colored race should be specially attracted. Through such association prejudice can be gradually eradicated, and 'Abdu'l-Bahá's ardent wish fully realized.
> On behalf of Shoghi Effendi, *Bahá'í News*, no. 103, 10/36, p. 1

49. Let him ["every would-be teacher of Bahá'u'lláh's Faith"] survey the possibilities which the particular circumstances in which he lives offer him, evaluate their advantages, and proceed intelligently and systematically to utilize them for the achievement of the object he has in mind. Let him also attempt to devise such methods as association with clubs, exhibitions, and societies, lectures on subjects akin to the

teachings and ideals of his Cause such as temperance, morality, social welfare, religion and racial tolerance, economic cooperation, Islam, and Comparative Religion, or participation in social, cultural, humanitarian, charitable, and educational organizations and enterprises which, while safeguarding the integrity of his Faith, will open up to him a multitude of ways and means whereby he can enlist successively the sympathy, the support, and ultimately the allegiance of those with whom he comes in contact.
Shoghi Effendi, *The Advent of Divine Justice*, pp. 42–43

50. The questions you have put to him are very pertinent and involve deep issues. The Negro race has been, and still is, the victim of unjust prejudice, and it is obviously the duty of every Bahá'í, Negro or white, to do all in their power to destroy the prejudices which exist on both sides. They can do this not only by exemplifying the true Bahá'í spirit in all their associations and acts, but also by taking an active part in any progressive movements aimed at the betterment of the lot of those who are underprivileged, as long as these movements are absolutely non-political and non-subversive in every respect....
On behalf of Shoghi Effendi, to an individual believer, 11/23/41

51. Fully aware of the repeated statements of 'Abdu'l-Bahá that universality is of God, Bahá'ís in every land are ready, nay anxious, to associate themselves by word and deed with any association of men which, after careful scrutiny, they feel satisfied is free from every tinge of partisanship and politics and is wholly devoted to the interests of all mankind. In their collaboration with such associations they would extend any moral and material assistance they can afford, after having fulfilled their share of support to those institutions that affect directly the interests of the Cause. They should always bear in mind, however, the dominating purpose of such a collabo-

ration which is to secure in time the recognition by those with whom they are associated of the paramount necessity and the true significance of the Bahá'í Revelation in this day.
> Shoghi Effendi, *Bahá'í Administration*, pp. 125–26

52. Much as the friends must guard against in any way ever seeming to identify themselves or the Cause with any political party, they must also guard against the other extreme of never taking part with other progressive groups, in conferences or committees designed to promote some activity in entire accord with our teachings—such as, for instance, better race relations.
> Shoghi Effendi, *Political Non-Involvement and Obedience to Government*, p. 29

53. In its letter of 23 January 1985 concerning the International Year of Peace, the Universal House of Justice urged Bahá'í communities to reach out to the non-Bahá'í public by finding ways of discussing the important issues of peace with others. One way to make such discussions relevant and effective is for the friends to know and acknowledge and pay just tribute to persons whose lives were dedicated to peaceful means of bettering social conditions.

One such person was the black American Martin Luther King, Jr. whose promotion of non-violent means of achieving racial equality in the United States cost him his life. The positive effects of his heroic efforts brought encouragement to downtrodden peoples throughout the world and earned him the Nobel Peace Prize in 1964. Four years later he was assassinated. His aspirations for a society in which the races can live in harmony are perhaps best expressed in the famous speech he delivered at a gathering of some 250,000 people in the capital of the United States in 1963. A copy is enclosed.

The House of Justice has asked us to call your attention to Dr. King for these reasons. His widow, Mrs. Coretta Scott King, a non-Bahá'í, has written to the House of Justice that a national public holiday has been officially designated in the United States in honor of Dr. King. She intends to make an appeal that on 20 January 1986, the first observance of this holiday, "nations and liberation movements all over the world cease all violent actions, seek amnesty and reconciliation both within and outside of their national boundaries, and encourage all of their citizens to recommit themselves to work for international peace, universal justice and the elimination of hunger and poverty in the world." The House of Justice feels that Mrs. King has a noble intention to which the friends can lend their moral and spiritual support. Since that date on which action is desired falls within the International Year of Peace, Spiritual Assemblies may consider holding peace conferences on 20 January, or close to that date, and naturally include in the presentations at these conferences references to the life and work of Dr. King. An alternative might be to devote the Bahá'í programs on World Religion Day, 19 January, to peace and on these occasions pay tribute to Dr. King.

The thought of the House of Justice in suggesting such action is not to promote the holiday for Dr. King, and it does not expect Bahá'í communities everywhere to commemorate his life annually; rather, it wishes to indicate to the friends a legitimate occasion, as illustrated by Mrs. King's plan, when the Bahá'í peace activities can be associated with the worthy activities of others.

We are to assure you of the continuing prayers of the House of Justice in the Holy Shrines that your energetic efforts to further the cause of peace throughout the earth may be richly confirmed by the Blessed Beauty.

<blockquote>The Universal House of Justice, to all National Spiritual Assemblies, 8/5/85</blockquote>

54. We understand that the Bahá'ís support the Martin Luther King Day in the United States primarily as an indication of its

encouragement of the upliftment of the black people in the United States and not necessarily as an effort to promote "the Martin Luther King movement." Similarly, 'Abdu'l-Bahá, during His visit to America, spoke before the fourth annual meeting of the National Association for the Advancement of Colored People (N.A.A.C.P.), which does not mean that he was supporting the explicit program of that particular organization, but rather, that he was affirming the principles which the N.A.A.C.P. seeks to uphold.
> On behalf of The Universal House of Justice, to an individual believer, 8/26/91

55. The entertainment given in honor of the National Association for advancement of colored people under the auspices of the National Bahá'í Interracial Committee assisted by the New York Spiritual Assembly seems to have been a most interesting meeting and highly beneficial to the cause of racial unity and peace. It is hoped that in the future meetings of this sort will increase both in number and in effectiveness.

Shoghi Effendi was deeply gratified to learn that you are slowly gaining the confidence of the leaders of the Colored people. He wishes you to persevere and to fearlessly proclaim the Bahá'í view point towards racial unity. For it is only in this way that you can promote the teachings of the Faith among the colored people.
> On behalf of Shoghi Effendi, to an individual believer, 6/3/33

56. Beyond attempting to provide an encouraging example of racial integration, the Bahá'í community in South Africa has devoted much of its energy to the inculcation of Bahá'í principles related to the oneness of mankind and on the development of a sense of self-worth and of social responsibility in the individual. Parallel with these activities has been a program aimed at training Spiritual Assemblies in principles of consultation and problem-solving. Bahá'ís are

particularly proud of the results of this effort because through it black believers have assumed the highest elective and appointive offices in the community.

This historical background points up the Bahá'í conviction that solutions to situations such as that which prevails in South Africa must draw on the force of example. Fundamental changes in social attitude will be most readily achieved if the relevant spiritual and moral principles are courageously set forth and if men and women of good will can see others attempting successfully to give these ideals practical expression in individual and community life.

>The Universal House of Justice, *Apartheid: A Bahá'í View*, to all National Spiritual Assemblies, 10/12/86

57. The Universal House of Justice sympathizes with your view that the situation in America has not changed as hoped, but as the beloved Guardian has told us in the *Advent of Divine Justice*, no profound and lasting change will come about unless certain spiritual prerequisites are met. These prerequisites have yet to be achieved by the broad public, and Bahá'ís themselves have often been slow to put them into practice.

Your suggestion that some form of anthropology should be taught to all children is a good one, because when young people have access to accurate, biological information, when they learn how amorphous and uncertain such terms as "race" have been in terms of their precise scientific usage, this information will tend to inoculate them against some of the cruder, but nevertheless insidious, arguments used by racists to bolster their positions. Indeed, we should welcome any sound method for removing the encumbrances to a fruitful effort in resolving racial prejudices.

That the term "race", as used in its ordinary sense to describe one of the major, broad divisions of mankind, should be substituted by a new word, is interesting, but it will be hard to judge at this stage the effectiveness of such a change in view of the history of other changes within our own lifetimes. For instance, as pointed out in your letter, among the black people in the United States, the adjective of choice has changed from colored to Negro, to black, to Afro-American to African-American, and still no resolution has been reached in determining a universally acceptable and appropriate terminology for describing the race. This demonstrates really that the results sought are less inherent in terminologies than in the transformation of hearts which will be brought about only through the power of the Blessed Beauty and in the manner described by the beloved Guardian.

Your continuing, thoughtful efforts to find ways of alleviating the dissensions afflicting the peoples of America are appreciated by the House of Justice; you may be assured that it will pray ardently in the Holy Shrines that Bahá'u'lláh may confirm your efforts in the path of unity.
> The Universal House of Justice,
> to an individual believer, 5/23/90

V. Conferences and Committees

> *It is especially gratifying to see the results of the Amity Conferences*
> *for a better spirit of fellowship and brotherliness. . . .*
> Shoghi Effendi

> *The beloved Guardian feels that sufficient attention is not being paid*
> *to the matter of contacting minorities in the United States . . .*
> *He feels your Assembly should appoint a special committee*
> *to survey the possibilities of this kind of work. . . .*
> Shoghi Effendi

58. The importance of this [racial amity] work cannot be overestimated by the American believers. In February, 1921, Mr. Mountford Mills took the following notes from words of

'Abdu'l-Bahá on the subject of the . . . Amity Convention in Washington, D.C.: "Unless this problem were solved, before long there would break out a terrible conflict in the United States between these two races that would be devastating in its effect. Say to this Convention that never since the beginning of time has one more important been held. This Convention stands for the oneness of humanity; it will become the cause of the removal of hostility between races; it will be the cause of the enlightenment of America. It will, if wisely managed and continued, check the deadly struggle between these races which otherwise will inevitably break out."

Bahá'í News, no. 16, 3/27, p. 5

59. Concerning the racial amity conferences; the Guardian firmly believes that they constitute a vital and inseparable part of the teaching campaign now being carried on by the American believers. It is the duty of every loyal Bahá'í to do all that he possibly can to promote this phase of Bahá'í activity, without which no campaign of teaching can bear lasting results.

On behalf of Shoghi Effendi,
to an individual believer, 11/11/36

60. You mentioned the Unity Conferences that were held there some time ago. This is a new and very promising plan for teaching the Cause to broad-minded and progressive people. The friends should do their level best to make this a success and try to bring definitely in the Cause persons attracted to the teachings through those meetings. Shoghi Effendi has great hopes in this new system of teaching and earnestly prays for its success. One thing to bear in mind is that the preparation for these Conferences and the work after them are very important and need great care before any result can be obtained.

On behalf of Shoghi Effendi, to an individual believer, 12/15/26

61. The work of the Race Unity Committee should include, as far as is possible, contacts with all minority groups, and wherever there is a particularly stout prejudice against a special group—such as the feelings against the Japanese in the Western States and the Negroes in the Southern (states), etc., efforts should be made to counteract it by showing publicly the Bahá'í example of loving tolerance and brotherly association.
   On behalf of Shoghi Effendi, *Bahá'í News*, no. 188, 10/46, pp. 3–4

62. It is especially gratifying to see the results of the Amity Conferences for a better spirit of fellowship and brotherliness among the colored and the white. This is a field where the Bahá'ís on both sides must show in actual deeds and actions the result of the principles and teachings of the Cause. He hopes that you will, in this connection be able to render great services.
   On behalf of Shoghi Effendi,
   to an individual believer, 5/23/27

63. Your warm and welcome message of Sept. 11, 1933, together with the enclosed reports and program of the annual conference for racial amity at Green Acre, were all duly received and their perusal greatly cheered and gladdened our Guardian's heart. His hope is that these annual gatherings will increasingly develop, and will serve to attract well known and important personalities to the Cause. Competent and eloquent speakers are needed who can present the teachings in a scholarly way, and who cannot merely inform, but inspire the attendants to rally themselves under the banner of the Faith. The keen and continued interest which Mr. Vail and yourself have always had in such activities will undoubtedly be of immense help to the cause of Racial Amity and peace throughout the States. You should therefore per-

severe and be confident in the complete and eventual success of your efforts in this most important field of activity.
>On behalf of Shoghi Effendi, 10/24/33, to an individual believer, *Bahá'í News*, no. 80, 1/34, p. 7

64. Also . . . the Faith must be representative of the population. In a great many places in the South, the majority of the population is still Negro. This should be reflected in the Bahá'í Community, fearlessly. Both the white Bahá'ís and the colored Bahá'ís must steadily work to attain this objective of bringing the Faith to the colored people, and of confirming many of them in it. Both sides have prejudices to overcome....

Your committee should devote the major part of its effort towards attaining these goals in the South, and it should also as part of its work, urge the Bahá'ís, wherever they may be, to devote more attention to the minorities.
>On behalf of Shoghi Effendi, to the Inter-Racial Teaching Committee, in *To Move the World*, p. 294

65. Freedom from racial prejudice . . . should be deliberately cultivated through the various and everyday opportunities, no matter how insignificant, that present themselves, whether in their homes, their business offices, their schools and colleges, their social parties and recreation grounds, their Bahá'í meetings, conferences, conventions, summer schools and Assemblies.
>Shoghi Effendi, *The Advent of Divine Justice*, p. 30

66. The beloved Guardian feels that sufficient attention is not being paid to the matter of contacting minorities in the United States. . . . He feels your Assembly should appoint a special committee to survey the possibilities of this kind of work, and then instruct local Assemblies accordingly, and in the meantime encourage the Bahá'ís to be active in this field, which is one open to everybody, as the minorities are invari-

ably lonely, and often respond to kindness much more quickly than the well-established majority of the population.
On behalf of Shoghi Effendi, in *The Priceless Pearl*, p. 368

67. Shoghi Effendi stressed that the obstacles that were preventing blacks from becoming Bahá'ís in greater numbers must be removed—"not for the sake of the Colored Group, but, for the sake of the whole well being and harmony and safety of the world, and for the sake of establishing the Kingdom of God on earth." Race prejudice was "America's vital problem," but it was not simply a matter of national concern: "Shoghi Effendi says that the tranquility of all the peoples of the earth depends on this one thing, the coming together of the White and the Black." The Bahá'ís must play a pivotal role in the solution of this problem, he told her. In order to begin to assume this role "the Negro [must] be represented, that he might express his viewpoint, that you might understand his position; that we might reach across this chasm. . . . " Therefore, every Bahá'í committee should have at least one black member, he emphasized, even if the same individual had to be appointed "over and over again." Above all, every effort should be made to open the door for large numbers of black people to enter the Cause.
To Move the World, p. 179

68. She [Dorothy Baker] shared with the audience of over two thousand Bahá'ís a theme that Shoghi Effendi had reiterated during her recent pilgrimage. "He said one driving thing over and over—that if we did not meet the challenging requirement of raising to a vast number the believers of the Negro race, disasters would result. And second," she continued, "that it was now for us to arise and reach the Indians of this country. In fact he went so far as to say on two occasions that this dual task is the most important teaching work on American shores today."

The problem of achieving racial unity, as both Shoghi Effendi and 'Abdu'l-Bahá had always intimated, was not simply national in scope. As Dorothy Baker reported it, it was clearly related to a general shift in the balance of power from the old colonial regimes to their former subjects:

"Now the dark-skinned people, he said, would have an upsurge that is both spiritual and social. The spiritual upsurge will rapidly bring them great gifts because this is an act of God, and it is so intended. And all the world's prejudiced forces will not hold it back one hair's breadth. The Bahá'ís will glorify it and understand it. The social repercussions of race suppressions around the world will increase at the same time, and, frightened, the world's forces will see that the dark-skinned peoples are really rising to the top—a cream that has latent gifts only to be brought out by divine bounties.

"Where do the Bahá'ís stand in this? Again and again he pointed out that the Bahá'ís must be in the vanguard of finding them and giving them the Faith. For the social repercussions will at times become dreadful if we do not, and we shall be judged by God.

"I thought that I was rather a fanatic on the race question—at least a strong liberal. But I sat there judged by my Guardian, and I knew it. My sights were lifted immeasurably....

"God forbid that even in this coming year we fail in this. And the first solution is offered us by the Guardian. He wishes the appointment of two important national committees immediately. One is to reach the Negro minority of America with this great truth in vast numbers. Not just little publicity stunts either, but to make them believers. The second committee is to reach the Indian tribes of this continent. And some of us, to draw out further light on the subject, even questioned a great deal about the kind of psychology that might ensue if you had a committee just to reach the Negroes. But he rather scoffed at it, in a precious, twinkling

kind of way, and firmly reiterated that without such special attention we simply had not done it—and that the important thing is to do it."
   To Move the World, pp. 292–93

69. Concerning the particular questions posed in your letter ... about the special committee called for by Shoghi Effendi to assist with teaching of African Americans, this and the race unity committee are undoubtedly one and the same. Conferences designed specifically for one particular ethnic group may or may not be advisable, depending on the particular context and situation in which they are to occur. Therefore, the decision whether or not to hold such a meeting would normally fall within the discretion of the National Spiritual Assembly, which, being closer to the scene, is in the best position to determine the advisability of such meetings.
   The Universal House of Justice,
   to an individual believer, 1/10/95

70. If we allow prejudice of any kind to manifest itself in us, we shall be guilty before God of causing a setback to the progress and real growth of the Faith of Bahá'u'lláh. It is incumbent upon every believer to endeavor with a fierce determination to eliminate this defect from his thoughts and acts. It is the duty of the institutions of the Faith to inculcate this principle in the hearts of the friends through every means at their disposal including summer schools, conferences, institutes and study classes.
   The Universal House of Justice, *Messages from The Universal House of Justice,* p. 100

71. These [racial problems, especially between Whites and Blacks, in southern California] have brought back to mind the warnings and advice of 'Abdu'l-Bahá and Shoghi Effendi concerning the racial situation in the United States which is

far from having been resolved. In this regard the House of Justice appreciates the attention you are attempting to give to this situation by your appointment each year of a Race Unity Committee; however, it has noticed that 'Abdu'l-Bahá's advice concerning the holding of Race Amity Conferences is not being systematically followed. You are asked, therefore, to give the most careful consideration to reviving the Race Amity Conferences as a regular feature among the activities of your national community. Los Angeles would, of course, qualify as a venue for any such conference.
> On behalf of The Universal House of Justice, to the
> National Spiritual Assembly of the Bahá'ís of the United States,
> 1/14/87

VI. African Americans as Pioneers

> *It has been a great step forward*
> *in the Cause's development in America*
> *to have Negro pioneers go forth,*
> *and their work has been of the greatest help*
> *and very productive of results.*
> Shoghi Effendi

72. They that have forsaken their country for the purpose of teaching Our Cause—these shall the Faithful Spirit strengthen through its power. A company of Our chosen angels shall go forth with them, as bidden by Him Who is the Almighty, the All-Wise. How great the blessedness that awaiteth him that hath attained the honor of serving the Almighty! By My life! No act, however great, can compare with it, except such deeds as have been ordained by God, the All-Powerful, the Most Mighty. Such a service is, indeed, the prince of all goodly deeds, and the ornament of every goodly act.
> Bahá'u'lláh, *Gleanings*, p. 334

73. O that I could travel, even though on foot and in the utmost poverty, to these regions, and, raising the call of "Yá Bahá'u'l-Abhá" in cities, villages, mountains, deserts and oceans, promote the Divine teachings! This, alas, I cannot do. How intensely I implore it! Please God, ye may achieve it.
'Abdu'l-Bahá, *Tablets of the Divine Plan*, p. 39

74. Now is the time for you to divest yourselves of the garment of attachment to this world that perisheth, to be wholly severed from the physical world, become heavenly angels, and travel to these countries. I swear by Him besides Whom there is none other God that each one of you will become an Isráfíl of Life, and will blow the Breath of Life into the souls of others.
'Abdu'l-Bahá, *Tablets of the Divine Plan*, p. 34

75. I fervently hope that in the near future the whole earth may be stirred and shaken by the results of your achievements.
'Abdu'l-Bahá, *Tablets of the Divine Plan*, p. 38

76. Exert yourselves; your mission is unspeakably glorious.
'Abdu'l-Bahá, *Tablets of the Divine Plan*, p. 73

77. Feel moved to appeal to gallant, great-hearted American Bahá'í Community to arise on the eve of launching the far-reaching, historic campaign by sister Community of the British Isles to lend valued assistance to the meritorious enterprise undertaken primarily for the illumination of the tribes of East and West Africa, envisaged in the Tablets of the Center of the Covenant revealed in the darkest hour of His ministry.

I appeal particularly to its dearly beloved members belonging to the Negro race to participate in the contemplated project marking a significant milestone in the world-unfoldment of the Faith. . . .

Though such participation is outside the scope of the Second Seven Year Plan, I feel strongly that the assumption of this added responsibility for this distant vital field at this crucial challenging hour, when world events are moving steadily towards a climax and the Centenary of the birth of Bahá'u'lláh's Mission is fast approaching, will further ennoble the record of the world-embracing tasks valiantly undertaken by the American Bahá'í Community and constitute a worthy response to 'Abdu'l-Bahá's insistent call raised on behalf of the race He repeatedly blessed and loved so dearly and for whose illumination He ardently prayed and for whose future He cherished the brightest hopes.
Shoghi Effendi, *Citadel of Faith*, p. 87

78. He was very pleased to have the first pioneer from America go forth under this organized African campaign; he was doubly happy that it should have been an American Negro who went. This is highly appropriate and surely has delighted the heart of 'Abdu'l-Bahá who watched over that race with particular love, tenderness and understanding. The ever-increasing part the colored friends are taking in the work of the Cause, and especially of late years in the pioneer work, gratifies the Guardian immensely. And now, to add further to the record of their services, they can count a member of their race a Hand of the Cause. When we read in the Will and Testament how great is the function of the Hands, we appreciate to what an exalted station our dear brother Louis Gregory attained.

The Guardian hopes that now the American Bahá'ís have arisen and started on their pioneer work in Africa they will go on with it at an accelerated pace.
On behalf of Shoghi Effendi, *Bahá'í News*, no. 252, 2/52, p. 1

79. The Negro believers must be just as active as their white brothers and sisters in spreading the Faith, both among their

own race and members of other races. It has been a great step forward in the Cause's development in America to have Negro pioneers go forth, and their work has been of the greatest help and very productive of results.
    On behalf of Shoghi Effendi, *Lights of Guidance*, p. 402

80. He would like your committee to convey to all the pioneers, most particularly the Negro ones, the expression of his deep admiration of the wonderful spirit that animates them, his feeling of affection for them, and the assurance of his ardent prayers for their success.

    Africa is truly awakening and finding herself, and she undoubtedly has a great message to give, and a great contribution to make to the advancement of world civilization. To the degree to which her peoples accept Bahá'u'lláh, will they be blessed, strengthened and protected.
    On behalf of Shoghi Effendi, *Unfolding Destiny*, p. 330

81. The decision you have taken to go to Africa and teach the Cause is momentous and is worthy of the great race you belong to. The Guardian has been eagerly awaiting a Negro pioneer, and feels that Bahá'u'lláh will surely bless your enterprise and assist you in this work you are planning for His Faith.
    On behalf of Shoghi Effendi, *Bahá'í News*, no. 247, 9/51, p. 1

82. Of all the places in the world where the Bahá'í Faith exists and is spreading, the Guardian is definitely most pleased with Africa, and most proud of Uganda. He feels that the spirit shown by white and Negro pioneers alike in that continent, presents a challenge to Bahá'ís everywhere in the world, and that old and staid communities may well learn from, and emulate the example of, the believers in Africa, many of them scarcely a year old in the Cause of God!
    On behalf of Shoghi Effendi, *Unfolding Destiny*, p. 329

83. He wishes you all every success in your work, and considers you are one of the most vital committees functioning in the Bahá'í work.

Every effort should be made to get as many pioneers out to Africa as possible and as soon as possible.
On behalf of Shoghi Effendi, to the Africa Committee, 9/7/51

84. He was most happy to hear that you are willing and eager to go out to Africa as pioneers, and it would give him great joy to see you both serving the Faith there.

He advises you to contact the Africa Committee, and, in consultation with them, see where your services would be of the most value. As you know, racial prejudice in some countries of Africa is growing at a most rapid pace; and the very fact that in your marriage, you exemplify our complete lack of racial feeling, might in itself be an irritant in some countries, and might assist in other countries. No doubt the Committee, who is studying this matter thoroughly, in conjunction with the British Africa Committee, will give you sound advice and help.
On behalf of Shoghi Effendi, to individual believers, 1/30/52

85. The country of Africa is surging with new life; and the friends should go there to assist in the awakening of that great continent.
On behalf of Shoghi Effendi, 12/14/55

86. Although not many pioneers can go out at once to Africa, all Bahá'ís can help ... by working more actively at home to break down racial barriers, and to foster loving association with minority groups. The Bahá'ís should go out amongst such groups and include them in their activities as much as possible.
On behalf of Shoghi Effendi, *The Power of Unity*, p. 105

87. The greater the love, harmony, and spirit of complete and selfless dedication which animates the members of a spiritual assembly, the greater will be the degree of Divine inspiration and assistance vouchsafed to them. Pioneer service in these epoch-making days need not be confined to going out in foreign fields. The friends can pioneer on their assemblies in helping to bring about a keener vision of what their duties are; they can pioneer in developing new local teaching methods, new contacts with new classes of people; indeed they can even be said to pioneer inwardly in finding new depths in their own souls and new ways in which their own God-given capacities can be put to use in serving the Faith.
    On behalf of Shoghi Effendi, to an individual believer, 7/8/42

88. He has spoken very strongly to some of the pilgrims here about the teaching work in that country, and impressed upon them that the whole object of the pioneers in going forth to Africa, is to teach the colored people; and not the white people. This does not mean that they must refuse to teach the white people, which would be a foolish attitude. It does, however, mean that they should constantly bear in mind that it is to the native African that they are now carrying the Message of Bahá'u'lláh, in his own country, and not to people from abroad who have migrated there permanently or temporarily and are a minority, and many of them, judging by their acts, a very unsavory minority.
    On behalf of Shoghi Effendi, *Unfolding Destiny*, p. 330

89. You have voiced the same suffering, the sign of the same mystery, as has been voiced by almost all those who have been called upon to serve God. Even the Prophets of God, we know, suffered agony when the Spirit of God descended on

Them and commanded Them to arise and preach. Look at Moses saying, "I am a stutterer!" Look at Muḥammad rolled in His rug in agony! The Guardian himself suffered terribly when he learned he was the one who had been made the Guardian.

So you see your sense of inadequacy, your realization of your own unworthiness is not unique at all. Many, from the Highest to the humblest have had it. Now the wisdom of it is this: it is such seemingly weak instruments that demonstrate that God is the Power achieving the victories and not men. If you were a wealthy, prominent, strong individual who knew all about Africa and looked upon going out there as fun, any service you render, and victories you have, would be laid to your personality, not to the Cause of God! But because the reverse is true, your services will be a witness to the Power of Bahá'u'lláh and Truth of His Faith.

Rest assured, dear sister, you will ever-increasingly be sustained, and you will find joy and strength given to you, and God will reward you. You will pass through these dark hours triumphant. The first Bahá'í going on such an historic mission could not but suffer—but the compensation will be great. . . .

On behalf of Shoghi Effendi, *Unfolding Destiny*, p. 459

90. Many of the gravest ills now afflicting the human race appear in acute form on the African Continent. Racial, tribal and religious prejudice, disunity of nations, the scourge of political factionalism, poverty and lack of education are obvious examples. Bahá'ís have a great part to play—greater than they may realize—in the healing of these sicknesses and the abatement of their worst effects. By their radiant unity, by their "bright and shining" faces, their self-discipline in zealously following all the requirements of Bahá'í law, their abstention from politics, their constant study and proclama-

tion of the Great Message, they will hasten the advent of that glorious day when all mankind will know its true brotherhood and will bask in the sunshine of God's love and blessing.

That the African believers are fully capable of taking their full share in building the Kingdom of God on earth, their natural abilities and present deeds have fully demonstrated....
> The Universal House of Justice, *Messages from The Universal House of Justice*, pp. 62–63

91. The Universal House of Justice was touched by the spirit of your letter ... and we are to assure you of its loving prayers at the Holy Threshold for the confirmation of your aspirations in service to the Cause of God. Unquestionably, the African-American believers are enviably poised to bring the life-giving Teachings of Bahá'u'lláh to persons of African heritage living in the United States, as well as to the peoples of sub-Saharan Africa itself, with whom they share a common ancestry. Shoghi Effendi specially encouraged black American believers to pioneer to Africa, and there have been some who heeded that call, serving the Cause with great distinction and to great effect. But many more are needed.

Be assured that the House of Justice will also pray for the success of your teaching efforts, in which it is keenly interested.
> On behalf of The Universal House of Justice, to individual believers, 2/14/94

92. We direct the attention of the believers of African descent, so beloved by the Master, to the pressing need for pioneers, who will contribute to the future development of the Cause in distant areas, including the continent of Africa for which they were assigned a special responsibility by the Guardian when the first systematic campaign was launched for its spiritual illumination. Although their contributions to all aspects of Bahá'í service on the home front and elsewhere

will be of great value, they can be a unique source of encouragement and inspiration to their African brothers and sisters who are now poised on the threshold of great advances for the Faith of Bahá'u'lláh.
> The Universal House of Justice, To the Followers of Bahá'u'lláh in North America: Alaska, Canada, Greenland and the United States, Riḍván 153

Seven

Destiny

> *Were man to appreciate the greatness of his station*
> *and the loftiness of his destiny*
> *he would manifest naught save goodly character, pure deeds,*
> *and a seemly and praiseworthy conduct. . . .*
> *This servant appealeth to every diligent and enterprising soul*
> *to exert his utmost endeavor*
> *and arise to rehabilitate the conditions in all regions*
> *and to quicken the dead with the living waters of wisdom and utterance,*
> *by virtue of the love he cherisheth for God,*
> *the One, the Peerless, the Almighty, the Beneficent.*
> Tablets of Bahá'u'lláh, p.172

1. Verily the faces of these [the members of the black race] are as the pupil of the eye; although the pupil is created black, yet it is the source of light. I hope God will make these black ones the glory of the white ones and as the wellspring of the light of love of God. And I ask God to assist them under all circumstances, that they may be encompassed with the favors of their Loving Lord throughout centuries and ages.
    'Abdu'l-Bahá, *The Power of Unity*, p. 69

2. The Guardian is very happy over the activities of the friends throughout Africa. That great continent is now becoming alive, and will certainly take its place in the forefront of Bahá'í communities.
    On behalf of Shoghi Effendi, 5/15/53

3. . . . the people of Africa, especially those who become Bahá'ís, have wonderful characteristics which, when pooled

with those of other nations and races, will greatly enrich our joint human heritage.
>Shoghi Effendi, to an individual believer, 8/9/54

4. The Negroes, though they themselves may not realize it, have a contribution to make to the World Order of Bahá'u'lláh. His teachings and the Society He has come to establish are for every race and every nation, and each one of them has his own part to play and the gift of his own qualities and talents to give to the whole.
>On behalf of Shoghi Effendi, *The Power of Unity*, pp. 77–78

5. Now the dark-skinned people, he [Shoghi Effendi] said, would have an upsurge that is both spiritual and social. The spiritual upsurge will rapidly bring them great gifts because this is an act of God, and it is so intended. And all the world's prejudiced forces will not hold it back one hair's breadth. The Bahá'ís will glorify it and understand it. The social repercussions of race suppressions around the world will increase at the same time, and, frightened, the world's forces will see that the dark-skinned peoples are really rising to the top—a cream that has latent gifts only to be brought out by divine bounties.
>*To Move the World*, p. 292

6. In the future the Cause of God will spread throughout America; millions will be enlisted under its banner and race prejudice will finally be exorcised from the body politic. Of this have no doubt. It is inexorable, because it is the Will of Almighty God.
>On behalf of The Universal House of Justice, to an individual believer, 4/1/96

7. Among some of the most momentous and thought-provoking pronouncements ever made by 'Abdu'l-Bahá, in the course of His epoch-making travels in the Northern Ameri-

can continent, are the following: *"May this American Democracy be the first nation to establish the foundation of international agreement. My it be the first nation to proclaim the unity of mankind. May it be the first to unfurl the Standard of the Most Great Peace."* And again: *"The American people are indeed worthy of being the first to build the Tabernacle of the Great Peace, and proclaim the oneness of mankind. . . . For America hath developed powers and capacities greater and more wonderful than other nations. . . . The American nation is equipped and empowered to accomplish that which will adorn the pages of history, to become the envy of the world, and be blest in both the East and the West for the triumph of its people. . . . The American continent gives signs and evidences of very great advancement. Its future is even more promising, for its influence and illumination are far-reaching. It will lead all nations spiritually."*
    The Advent of Divine Justice, p. 72

8. One word more in conclusion. The proclamation of the Oneness of Mankind—the head cornerstone of Bahá'u'lláh's all-embracing dominion—can under no circumstances be compared with such expressions of pious hope as have been uttered in the past. His is not merely a call which He raised, alone and unaided, in the face of the relentless and combined opposition of two of the most powerful Oriental potentates of His day—while Himself an exile and prisoner in their hands. It implies at once a warning and a promise—a warning that in it lies the sole means for the salvation of a greatly suffering world, a promise that its realization is at hand.
    Uttered at a time when its possibility had not yet been seriously envisaged in any part of the world, it has, by virtue of that celestial potency which the Spirit of Bahá'u'lláh has breathed into it, come at last to be regarded, by an increasing number of thoughtful men, not only as an approaching possibility, but as the necessary outcome of the forces now operating in the world.
    Shoghi Effendi, *The World Order of Bahá'u'lláh*, p. 47

9. Not ours, puny mortals that we are, to attempt, at so critical a stage in the long and checkered history of mankind, to arrive at a precise and satisfactory understanding of the steps which must successively lead a bleeding humanity, wretchedly oblivious of its God, and careless of Bahá'u'lláh, from its calvary to its ultimate resurrection. Not ours, the living witnesses of the all-subduing potency of His Faith, to question, for a moment, and however dark the misery that enshrouds the world, the ability of Bahá'u'lláh to forge, with the hammer of His Will, and through the fire of tribulation, upon the anvil of this travailing age, and in the particular shape His mind has envisioned, these scattered and mutually destructive fragments into which a perverse world has fallen, into one single unit, solid and indivisible, able to execute His design for the children of men.

Ours rather the duty, however confused the scene, however dismal the present outlook, however circumscribed the resources we dispose of, to labor serenely, confidently, and unremittingly to lend our share of assistance, in whichever way circumstances may enable us, to the operation of the forces which, as marshaled and directed by Bahá'u'lláh, are leading humanity out of the valley of misery and shame to the loftiest summits of power and glory.

Shoghi Effendi, *The Promised Day Is Come*, p. 124

10. What we witness at the present time, during "this gravest crisis in the history of civilization," recalling such times in which "religions have perished and are born," is the adolescent stage in the slow and painful evolution of humanity, preparatory to the attainment of the stage of manhood, the stage of maturity, the promise of which is embedded in the teachings, and enshrined in the prophecies, of Bahá'u'lláh. The tumult of this age of transition is characteristic of the impetuosity and irrational instincts of youth, its follies, its prodigality, its pride, its self-assurance, its rebelliousness, and contempt of discipline.

The ages of its infancy and childhood are past, never again to return, while the Great Age, the consummation of all ages, which must signalize the coming of age of the entire human race, is yet to come. The convulsions of this transitional and most turbulent period in the annals of humanity are the essential prerequisites, and herald the inevitable approach, of that Age of Ages, "the time of the end," in which the folly and tumult of strife that has, since the dawn of history, blackened the annals of mankind, will have been finally transmuted into the wisdom and the tranquility of an undisturbed, a universal, and lasting peace, in which the discord and separation of the children of men will have given way to the worldwide reconciliation, and the complete unification of the divers elements that constitute human society.

This will indeed be the fitting climax of that process of integration which, starting with the family, the smallest unit in the scale of human organization, must, after having called successively into being the tribe, the city-state, and the nation, continue to operate until it culminates in the unification of the whole world, the final object and the crowning glory of human evolution on this planet. It is this stage which humanity, willingly or unwillingly, is resistlessly approaching. It is for this stage that this vast, this fiery ordeal which humanity is experiencing is mysteriously paving the way. It is with this stage that the fortunes and the purpose of the Faith of Bahá'u'lláh are indissolubly linked.

Shoghi Effendi, *The Promised Day is Come*, pp. 121–22

11. One of the great events . . . which is to occur in the Day of the manifestation of that incomparable Branch is the hoisting of the Standard of God among all nations. By this is meant that all nations and kindreds will be gathered together under the shadow of this Divine Banner, which is no other than the Lordly Branch itself, and will become a single nation. Religious and sectarian antagonism, the hostility of races and peoples, and differences among nations, will be eliminated.

All men will adhere to one religion, will have one common faith, will be blended into one race and become a single people. All will dwell in one common fatherland, which is the planet itself.
'Abdu'l-Bahá, in *The World Order of Bahá'u'lláh*, pp. 204–05

12. In cycles gone by, though harmony was established, yet, owing to the absence of means, the unity of all mankind could not have been achieved. Continents remained widely divided, nay even among the peoples of one and the same continent association and interchange of thought were well nigh impossible. Consequently intercourse, understanding and unity amongst all the peoples and kindreds of the earth were unattainable. In this day, however, means of communication have multiplied, and the five continents of the earth have virtually merged into one. . . . In like manner all the members of the human family, whether peoples or governments, cities or villages, have become increasingly interdependent. For none is self-sufficiency any longer possible, inasmuch as political ties unite all peoples and nations, and the bonds of trade and industry, of agriculture and education, are being strengthened every day. Hence the unity of all mankind can in this day be achieved. Verily this is none other but one of the wonders of this wondrous age, this glorious century. Of this past ages have been deprived, for this century—the century of light—has been endowed with unique and unprecedented glory, power and illumination. Hence the miraculous unfolding of a fresh marvel every day. Eventually it will be seen how bright its candles will burn in the assemblage of man.

Behold how its light is now dawning upon the world's darkened horizon. The first candle is unity in the political realm, the early glimmerings of which can now be discerned. The second candle is unity of thought in world undertakings, the consummation of which will ere long be witnessed. The

third candle is unity in freedom which will surely come to pass. The fourth candle is unity in religion which is the cornerstone of the foundation itself, and which, by the power of God, will be revealed in all its splendor. The fifth candle is the unity of nations—a unity which in this century will be securely established, causing all the peoples of the world to regard themselves as citizens of one common fatherland. The sixth candle is unity of races, making of all that dwell on earth peoples and kindreds of one race. The seventh candle is unity of language, i.e., the choice of a universal tongue in which all peoples will be instructed and converse. Each and every one of these will inevitably come to pass, inasmuch as the power of the Kingdom of God will aid and assist in their realization.
    'Abdu'l-Bahá, in *The World Order of Bahá'u'lláh*, pp. 38–39

13. The world is, in truth, moving on towards its destiny. The interdependence of the peoples and nations of the earth, whatever the leaders of the divisive forces of the world may say or do, is already an accomplished fact. Its unity in the economic sphere is now understood and recognized. The welfare of the part means the welfare of the whole, and the distress of the part brings distress to the whole. The Revelation of Bahá'u'lláh has, in His own words, "lent a fresh impulse and set a new direction" to this vast process now operating in the world. The fires lit by this great ordeal are the consequences of men's failure to recognize it. They are, moreover, hastening its consummation. Adversity, prolonged, worldwide, afflictive, allied to chaos and universal destruction, must needs convulse the nations, stir the conscience of the world, disillusion the masses, precipitate a radical change in the very conception of society, and coalesce ultimately the disjointed, the bleeding limbs of mankind into one body, single, organically united, and indivisible.
    Shoghi Effendi, *The Promised Day Is Come*, pp. 122–23

14. This judgment of God, as viewed by those who have recognized Bahá'u'lláh as His Mouthpiece and His greatest Messenger on earth, is both a retributory calamity and an act of holy and supreme discipline. It is at once a visitation from God and a cleansing process for all mankind. Its fires punish the perversity of the human race, and weld its component parts into one organic, indivisible, world-embracing community. Mankind, in these fateful years, which at once signalize the passing of the first century of the Bahá'í Era and proclaim the opening of a new one, is, as ordained by Him Who is both the Judge and the Redeemer of the human race, being simultaneously called upon to give account of its past actions, and is being purged and prepared for its future mission. It can neither escape the responsibilities of the past, nor shirk those of the future. God, the Vigilant, the Just, the Loving, the All-Wise Ordainer, can, in this supreme Dispensation, neither allow the sins of an unregenerate humanity, whether of omission or of commission, to go unpunished, nor will He be willing to abandon His children to their fate, and refuse them that culminating and blissful stage in their long, their slow and painful evolution throughout the ages, which is at once their inalienable right and their true destiny.
    Shoghi Effendi, *The Promised Day Is Come*, pp. 2–3

15. God's purpose is none other than to usher in, in ways He alone can bring about, and the full significance of which He alone can fathom, the Great, the Golden Age of a long-divided, a long-afflicted humanity. Its present state, indeed even its immediate future, is dark, distressingly dark. Its distant future, however, is radiant, gloriously radiant—so radiant that no eye can visualize it.
    Shoghi Effendi, *The Promised Day Is Come*, p. 120

16. Then will the coming of age of the entire human race be proclaimed and celebrated by all the peoples and nations of the earth. Then will the banner of the Most Great Peace be hoisted. Then will the worldwide sovereignty of Bahá'u'lláh—the Establisher of the Kingdom of the Father foretold by the Son, and anticipated by the Prophets of God before Him and after Him—be recognized, acclaimed, and firmly established. Then will a world civilization be born, flourish, and perpetuate itself, a civilization with a fullness of life such as the world has never seen nor can as yet conceive. Then will the Everlasting Covenant be fulfilled in its completeness. Then will the promise enshrined in all the Books of God be redeemed, and all the prophecies uttered by the Prophets of old come to pass, and the vision of seers and poets be realized. Then will the planet, galvanized through the universal belief of its dwellers in one God, and their allegiance to one common Revelation, mirror, within the limitations imposed upon it, the effulgent glories of the sovereignty of Bahá'u'lláh, shining in the plenitude of its splendor in the Abhá Paradise, and be made the footstool of His Throne on high, and acclaimed as the earthly heaven, capable of fulfilling that ineffable destiny fixed for it, from time immemorial, by the love and wisdom of its Creator.

Shoghi Effendi, *The Promised Day Is Come*, pp. 128–29

Bibliography

'Abdu'l-Bahá in Canada, 1962.
The Advent of Divine Justice, 1963.
The American Bahá'í, 11/91
Arohanui—Letters from Shoghi Effendi to New Zealand, 1982.
Bahá'í Administration, 1968.
Bahá'í News, numbers 16, 18, 58, 80, 103, 105, 108, 157, 188, 210, 231, 238, 247, 251, 252, 321, 324, 333, 441.
The Bahá'í Revelation: A Selection from the Bahá'í Holy Writings, 1955.
The Bahá'í World, volumes VIII, XII, XVII, XVIII.
Bahá'í Youth: A Compilation, 1973.
Bahá'u'lláh and the New Era, 1980.
Citadel of Faith: Messages to America, 1947–1957, 1965.
Continental Boards of Counsellors, 1971.
Dawn of a New Day: Messages to India 1923–1957.
Developing Distinctive Bahá'í Communities: Guidelines for Spiritual Assemblies, 1989.
An Early Pilgrimage, 1917.
Epistle to the Son of the Wolf, 1962.
Excerpts from the Writings of the Guardian on The Bahá'í Life, 1974.
Foundations of World Unity: Compiled from Addresses and Tablets of 'Abdu'l-Bahá, 3rd printing, 1955.
Gleanings from the Writings of Bahá'u'lláh, , 3rd printing, 1963.
God Passes By, 1965.
The Hidden Words, reprinted 1985.
Ḥuqúqu'lláh: Extracts from the Writings of Bahá'u'lláh, 'Abdu'l-Bahá, Shoghi Effendi and The Universal House of Justice.
The Importance of Deepening our Knowledge and Understanding of the Faith. Canada, 1983.
The Individual and Teaching: Raising the Divine Call, 1977.
The Kitáb-i-Aqdas: The Most Holy Book, 1992.
The Kitáb-i-Íqán: The Book of Certitude, 1950.
Lights of Guidance: A Bahá'í Reference File, 1st ed., 1983.
Living the Life: A Compilation. London. Bahá'í Publishing Trust, 1974.
Messages from the Universal House of Justice, 1968–1973, 1976.
Messages from the Universal House of Justice, 1963–1986, 1996.
Messages to the Bahá'í World, 1950–1957, 1958.

To Move the World: Louis G. Gregory and the Advancement of Racial Unity in America, 1982.
Paris Talks, Addresses given by 'Abdu'l-Bahá in Paris in 1911–1912, 11th ed. 1969.
Political Non-Involvement and Obedience to Government, 1979.
The Power of Divine Assistance, 1982.
The Power of Unity: Beyond Prejudice and Racism, 1986.
The Priceless Pearl, 1969.
Principles of Bahá'í Administration: A Compilation, 1963.
Prayers and Meditations, 1962.
The Promised Day Is Come, 1967.
The Promise of World Peace: To the Peoples of the World, 1985.
The Promulgation of Universal Peace, Talks Delivered by 'Abdu'l-Bahá during His Visit to the United States and Canada in 1912, 2nd ed. 1982.
The Reality of Man: Excerpts from the Writings of Bahá'u'lláh and 'Abdu'l-Bahá, 1972.
The Secret of Divine Civilization, 1957.
Selections from the Writings of 'Abdu'l-Bahá, 1978.
Selections from the Writings of the Bab, 1976.
Some Answered Questions, 1964.
A Special Measure of Love: The Importance and Nature of the Teaching Work among the Masses, 1974.
Star of the West, volumes II, VIII, X, XII, XIII, reprinted July 1978.
Tablets of 'Abdu'l-Bahá, 2nd printing, 1930.
Tablets of Bahá'u'lláh revealed after the Kitab-i-Aqdas, 1978.
Tablets of the Divine Plan, 1977.
Unfolding Destiny: The Messages from the Guardian of the Bahá'í Faith to the Bahá'í Community of the British Isles, 1981.
Wellspring of Guidance, Messages 1963–1968, 1969.
Women, January 1986.
The World Order of Bahá'u'lláh, 1955.
World Order Through World Faith, 1946.